Cram101 Textbook Outlines to accompany:

The Theory of Interest

Kellison, 2nd Edition

An Academic Internet Publishers (AIPI) publication (c) 2007.

You have a discounted membership at www.Cram101.com with this book.

Get all of the practice tests for the chapters of this textbook, and access in-depth reference material for writing essays and papers. Here is an example from a Cram101 Biology text:

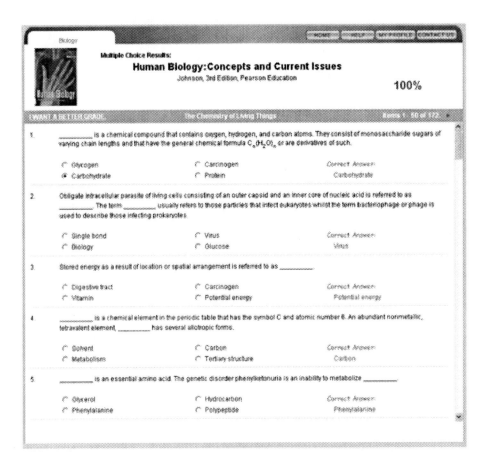

When you need problem solving help with math, stats, and other disciplines, www.Cram101.com will walk through the formulas and solutions step by step.

With Cram101.com online, you also have access to extensive reference material.

You will nail those essays and papers. Here is an example from a Cram101 Biology text:

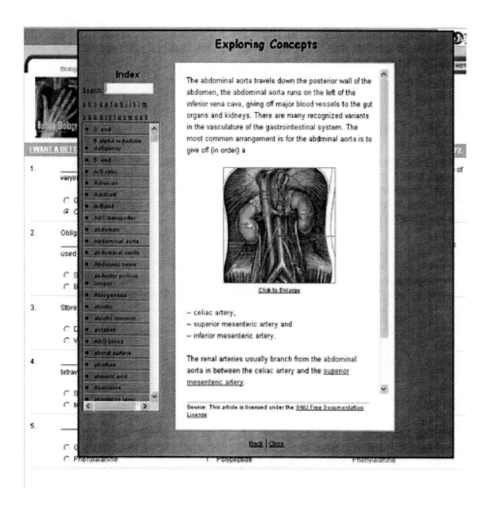

Visit **www.Cram101.com**, click Sign Up at the top of the screen, and enter DK73DW in the promo code box on the registration screen. Access to www.Cram101.com is normally $9.95, but because you have purchased this book, your access fee is only $4.95. Sign up and stop highlighting textbooks forever.

Learning System

Cram101 Textbook Outlines is a learning system. The notes in this book are the highlights of your textbook, you will never have to highlight a book again.

How to use this book. Take this book to class, it is your notebook for the lecture. The notes and highlights on the left hand side of the pages follow the outline and order of the textbook. All you have to do is follow along while your intructor presents the lecture. Circle the items emphasized in class and add other important information on the right side. With Cram101 Textbook Outlines you'll spend less time writing and more time listening. Learning becomes more efficient.

Cram101.com Online

Increase your studying efficiency by using Cram101.com's practice tests and online reference material. It is the perfect complement to Cram101 Textbook Outlines. Use self-teaching matching tests or simulate in-class testing with comprehensive multiple choice tests, or simply use Cram's true and false tests for quick review. Cram101.com even allows you to enter your in-class notes for an integrated studying format combining the textbook notes with your class notes.

Visit **www.Cram101.com**, click Sign Up at the top of the screen, and enter **DK73DW1564** in the promo code box on the registration screen. Access to www.Cram101.com is normally $9.95, but because you have purchased this book, your access fee is only $4.95. Sign up and stop highlighting textbooks forever.

The Theory of Interest
Kellison, 2nd

CONTENTS

Commodity	Could refer to any good, but in trade a commodity is usually a raw material or primary product that enters into international trade, such as metals or basic agricultural products.
Interest	In finance and economics, interest is the price paid by a borrower for the use of a lender's money. In other words, interest is the amount of paid to "rent" money for a period of time.
Capital	Capital generally refers to financial wealth, especially that used to start or maintain a business. In classical economics, capital is one of four factors of production, the others being land and labor and entrepreneurship.
Financial transaction	A financial transaction involves a change in the status of the finances of two or more businesses or individuals.
Investment	Investment refers to spending for the production and accumulation of capital and additions to inventories. In a financial sense, buying an asset with the expectation of making a return.
Accumulation	The acquisition of an increasing quantity of something. The accumulation of factors, especially capital, is a primary mechanism for economic growth.
Principal	In agency law, one under whose direction an agent acts and for whose benefit that agent acts is a principal.
Fund	Independent accounting entity with a self-balancing set of accounts segregated for the purposes of carrying on specific activities is referred to as a fund.
Contribution	In business organization law, the cash or property contributed to a business by its owners is referred to as contribution.
Points	Loan origination fees that may be deductible as interest by a buyer of property. A seller of property who pays points reduces the selling price by the amount of the points paid for the buyer.
Simple interest	Simple interest is interest that accrues linearly. In other words, it grows by a certain fraction of the principal per time period.
Derivative	A derivative is a generic term for specific types of investments from which payoffs over time are derived from the performance of assets (such as commodities, shares or bonds), interest rates, exchange rates, or indices (such as a stock market index, consumer price index (CPI) or an index of weather conditions).
Property	Assets defined in the broadest legal sense. Property includes the unrealized receivables of a cash basis taxpayer, but not services rendered.
Compound interest	Compound interest is interest computed on the sum of all past interest added as well as on the principal.
Balance	In banking and accountancy, the outstanding balance is the amount of money owned, (or due), that remains in a deposit account (or a loan account) at a given date, after all past remittances, payments and withdrawal have been accounted for. It can be positive (then, in the balance sheet of a firm, it is an asset) or negative (a liability).
Present value	The value today of a stream of payments and/or receipts over time in the future and/or the past, converted to the present using an interest rate. If X_t is the amount in period t and r the interest rate, then present value at time t=0 is $V = ?T /t$.
Accumulation factor	The value of n, in a future value calculation, where r denotes the interest rate per year and n denotes the number of years, is referred to as accumulation factor.
Discount	The difference between the face value of a bond and its selling price, when a bond is sold for less than its face value it's referred to as a discount.
Restatement	Restatement refers to collections of legal rules produced by the American Law Institute, covering certain subject matter areas. Although restatements are often persuasive to courts, they are not

Go to **Cram101.com** for the Practice Tests for this Chapter.

	legally binding unless adopted by the highest court of a particular state.
Discount factor	The discounted price is the original price multiplied by the discount factor.
Context	The effect of the background under which a message often takes on more and richer meaning is a context. Context is especially important in cross-cultural interactions because some cultures are said to be high context or low context.
Lender	Suppliers and financial institutions that lend money to companies is referred to as a lender.
Compounded semiannually	A compounding period of every six months is called compounded semiannually.
Conversion	Conversion refers to any distinct act of dominion wrongfully exerted over another's personal property in denial of or inconsistent with his rights therein. That tort committed by a person who deals with chattels not belonging to him in a manner that is inconsistent with the ownership of the lawful owner.
Frequency	Frequency refers to the speed of the up and down movements of a fluctuating economic variable; that is, the number of times per unit of time that the variable completes a cycle of up and down movement.
Nominal rate of interest	The nominal rate of interest is the percentage by which the money the borrower pays back exceeds the money that he borrowed, making no adjustment for any fall in the purchasing power of this money that results from inflation.
Interest rate	The rate of return on bonds, loans, or deposits. When one speaks of 'the' interest rate, it is usually in a model where there is only one.
Argument	The discussion by counsel for the respective parties of their contentions on the law and the facts of the case being tried in order to aid the jury in arriving at a correct and just conclusion is called argument.
Inflation	An increase in the overall price level of an economy, usually as measured by the CPI or by the implicit price deflator is called inflation.
Yield	The interest rate that equates a future value or an annuity to a given present value is a yield.
Bond	Bond refers to a debt instrument, issued by a borrower and promising a specified stream of payments to the purchaser, usually regular interest payments plus a final repayment of principal.
Slope	The slope of a line in the plane containing the x and y axes is generally represented by the letter m, and is defined as the change in the y coordinate divided by the corresponding change in the x coordinate, between two distinct points on the line.
Convergence	The blending of various facets of marketing functions and communication technology to create more efficient and expanded synergies is a convergence.
Appeal	Appeal refers to the act of asking an appellate court to overturn a decision after the trial court's final judgment has been entered.
Integration	Economic integration refers to reducing barriers among countries to transactions and to movements of goods, capital, and labor, including harmonization of laws, regulations, and standards. Integrated markets theoretically function as a unified market.
Discount rate	Discount rate refers to the rate, per year, at which future values are diminished to make them comparable to values in the present. Can be either subjective or objective .
Effective interest rate	Yield rate of bonds, which is usually equal to the market rate of interest on the day the bonds are sold is the effective interest rate.

Interest	In finance and economics, interest is the price paid by a borrower for the use of a lender's money. In other words, interest is the amount of paid to "rent" money for a period of time.
Financial transaction	A financial transaction involves a change in the status of the finances of two or more businesses or individuals.
Compound interest	Compound interest is interest computed on the sum of all past interest added as well as on the principal.
Simple interest	Simple interest is interest that accrues linearly. In other words, it grows by a certain fraction of the principal per time period.
Discount	The difference between the face value of a bond and its selling price, when a bond is sold for less than its face value it's referred to as a discount.
Investment	Investment refers to spending for the production and accumulation of capital and additions to inventories. In a financial sense, buying an asset with the expectation of making a return.
Lender	Suppliers and financial institutions that lend money to companies is referred to as a lender.
Principal	In agency law, one under whose direction an agent acts and for whose benefit that agent acts is a principal.
Present value	The value today of a stream of payments and/or receipts over time in the future and/or the past, converted to the present using an interest rate. If X t is the amount in period t and r the interest rate, then present value at time t=0 is V = ?T /t.
Complexity	The technical sophistication of the product and hence the amount of understanding required to use it is referred to as complexity. It is the opposite of simplicity.
Conversion	Conversion refers to any distinct act of dominion wrongfully exerted over another's personal property in denial of or inconsistent with his rights therein. That tort committed by a person who deals with chattels not belonging to him in a manner that is inconsistent with the ownership of the lawful owner.
Property	Assets defined in the broadest legal sense. Property includes the unrealized receivables of a cash basis taxpayer, but not services rendered.
Weighted average	The weighted average unit cost of the goods available for sale for both cost of goods sold and ending inventory.
Interest rate	The rate of return on bonds, loans, or deposits. When one speaks of 'the' interest rate, it is usually in a model where there is only one.
Rate of return	A rate of return is a comparison of the money earned (or lost) on an investment to the amount of money invested.
Advertisement	Advertisement is the promotion of goods, services, companies and ideas, usually by an identified sponsor. Marketers see advertising as part of an overall promotional strategy.
Certificate of deposit	An acknowledgment by a bank of the receipt of money with an engagement to pay it back is referred to as certificate of deposit.
Yield	The interest rate that equates a future value or an annuity to a given present value is a yield.
Money market	The money market, in macroeconomics and international finance, refers to the equilibration of demand for a country's domestic money to its money supply; market for short-term financial instruments.
Market	A market is, as defined in economics, a social arrangement that allows buyers and sellers to discover information and carry out a voluntary exchange of goods or services.

Go to **Cram101.com** for the Practice Tests for this Chapter.

Fund	Independent accounting entity with a self-balancing set of accounts segregated for the purposes of carrying on specific activities is referred to as a fund.
Frequency	Frequency refers to the speed of the up and down movements of a fluctuating economic variable; that is, the number of times per unit of time that the variable completes a cycle of up and down movement.
Trial	An examination before a competent tribunal, according to the law of the land, of the facts or law put in issue in a cause, for the purpose of determining such issue is a trial. When the court hears and determines any issue of fact or law for the purpose of determining the rights of the parties, it may be considered a trial.
Savings bank	A depository institution, owned by its depositors, that accepts savings deposits and makes mortgage loans is a savings bank.
Balance	In banking and accountancy, the outstanding balance is the amount of money owned, (or due), that remains in a deposit account (or a loan account) at a given date, after all past remittances, payments and withdrawal have been accounted for. It can be positive (then, in the balance sheet of a firm, it is an asset) or negative (a liability).
Credit	Credit refers to a recording as positive in the balance of payments, any transaction that gives rise to a payment into the country, such as an export, the sale of an asset, or borrowing from abroad.
Treasury bills	Short-term obligations of the federal government are treasury bills. They are like zero coupon bonds in that they do not pay interest prior to maturity; instead they are sold at a discount of the par value to create a positive yield to maturity.
Financial analysis	Financial analysis is the analysis of the accounts and the economic prospects of a firm.
Option	A contract that gives the purchaser the option to buy or sell the underlying financial instrument at a specified price, called the exercise price or strike price, within a specific period of time.
Nominal rate of interest	The nominal rate of interest is the percentage by which the money the borrower pays back exceeds the money that he borrowed, making no adjustment for any fall in the purchasing power of this money that results from inflation.
Savings and loan association	A financial institution that accepts both savings and checking deposits and provides home mortgage loans is referred to as savings and loan association.
Certificates of deposit	Certificates of deposit refer to a certificate offered by banks, savings and loans, and other financial institutions for the deposit of funds at a given interest rate over a specified time period.

Annuity	A contract to make regular payments to a person for life or for a fixed period is an annuity.
Property	Assets defined in the broadest legal sense. Property includes the unrealized receivables of a cash basis taxpayer, but not services rendered.
Conversion	Conversion refers to any distinct act of dominion wrongfully exerted over another's personal property in denial of or inconsistent with his rights therein. That tort committed by a person who deals with chattels not belonging to him in a manner that is inconsistent with the ownership of the lawful owner.
Interest	In finance and economics, interest is the price paid by a borrower for the use of a lender's money. In other words, interest is the amount of paid to "rent" money for a period of time.
Annuities	Financial contracts under which a customer pays an annual premium in exchange for a future stream of annual payments beginning at a set age, say 65, and ending when the person dies are annuities.
Present value	The value today of a stream of payments and/or receipts over time in the future and/or the past, converted to the present using an interest rate. If X t is the amount in period t and r the interest rate, then present value at time t=0 is V = ?T /t.
Clutter	The nonprogram material that appears in a broadcast environment, including commercials, promotional messages for shows, public service announcements, and the like is called clutter.
Interest rate	The rate of return on bonds, loans, or deposits. When one speaks of 'the' interest rate, it is usually in a model where there is only one.
Investment	Investment refers to spending for the production and accumulation of capital and additions to inventories. In a financial sense, buying an asset with the expectation of making a return.
Yield	The interest rate that equates a future value or an annuity to a given present value is a yield.
Interest payment	The payment to holders of bonds payable, calculated by multiplying the stated rate on the face of the bond by the par, or face, value of the bond. If bonds are issued at a discount or premium, the interest payment does not equal the interest expense.
Present value of an annuity	The sum of the present value of a series of consecutive equal payments is called present value of an annuity.
Principal	In agency law, one under whose direction an agent acts and for whose benefit that agent acts is a principal.
Fund	Independent accounting entity with a self-balancing set of accounts segregated for the purposes of carrying on specific activities is referred to as a fund.
Evaluation	The consumer's appraisal of the product or brand on important attributes is called evaluation.
Perpetuity	A perpetuity is an annuity in which the periodic payments begin on a fixed date and continue indefinitely. Fixed coupon payments on permanently invested (irredeemable) sums of money are prime examples of perpetuities. Scholarships paid perpetually from an endowment fit the definition of perpetuity.
Stock	In financial terminology, stock is the capital raized by a corporation, through the issuance and sale of shares.
Preferred stock	Stock that has specified rights over common stock is a preferred stock.
Argument	The discussion by counsel for the respective parties of their contentions on the law and the facts of the case being tried in order to aid the jury in arriving at a correct and just conclusion is called argument.

10

Go to **Cram101.com** for the Practice Tests for this Chapter.

Shares	Shares refer to an equity security, representing a shareholder's ownership of a corporation. Shares are one of a finite number of equal portions in the capital of a company, entitling the owner to a proportion of distributed, non-reinvested profits known as dividends and to a portion of the value of the company in case of liquidation.
Estate	An estate is the totality of the legal rights, interests, entitlements and obligations attaching to property. In the context of wills and probate, it refers to the totality of the property which the deceased owned or in which some interest was held.
Appeal	Appeal refers to the act of asking an appellate court to overturn a decision after the trial court's final judgment has been entered.
Balloon payment	Large final payment due at the maturity of a debt that otherwise requires systematic smaller payments over the term of the loan prior to maturity is a balloon payment.
Convergence	The blending of various facets of marketing functions and communication technology to create more efficient and expanded synergies is a convergence.
Trial	An examination before a competent tribunal, according to the law of the land, of the facts or law put in issue in a cause, for the purpose of determining such issue is a trial. When the court hears and determines any issue of fact or law for the purpose of determining the rights of the parties, it may be considered a trial.
Ad hoc	Ad hoc is a Latin phrase which means "for this purpose." It generally signifies a solution that has been tailored to a specific purpose and is makeshift and non-general, such as a handcrafted network protocol or a specific-purpose equation, as opposed to general solutions.
Accumulation	The acquisition of an increasing quantity of something. The accumulation of factors, especially capital, is a primary mechanism for economic growth.
Valuation	In finance, valuation is the process of estimating the market value of a financial asset or liability. They can be done on assets (for example, investments in marketable securities such as stocks, options, business enterprises, or intangible assets such as patents and trademarks) or on liabilities (e.g., Bonds issued by a company).
Compound interest	Compound interest is interest computed on the sum of all past interest added as well as on the principal.
Distortion	Distortion refers to any departure from the ideal of perfect competition that interferes with economic agents maximizing social welfare when they maximize their own.
Simple interest	Simple interest is interest that accrues linearly. In other words, it grows by a certain fraction of the principal per time period.
Balance	In banking and accountancy, the outstanding balance is the amount of money owned, (or due), that remains in a deposit account (or a loan account) at a given date, after all past remittances, payments and withdrawal have been accounted for. It can be positive (then, in the balance sheet of a firm, it is an asset) or negative (a liability).
Discount	The difference between the face value of a bond and its selling price, when a bond is sold for less than its face value it's referred to as a discount.
Benefactor	A benefactor is a person or other entity providing money or other benefits to another; the person receiving them is called a beneficiary.
Beneficiary	The person for whose benefit an insurance policy, trust, will, or contract is established is a beneficiary. In the case of a contract, the beneficiary is called a third-party beneficiary.
Insurance	Insurance refers to a system by which individuals can reduce their exposure to risk of large losses by spreading the risks among a large number of persons.

| **Effective interest rate** | Yield rate of bonds, which is usually equal to the market rate of interest on the day the bonds are sold is the effective interest rate. |
| **Discount rate** | Discount rate refers to the rate, per year, at which future values are diminished to make them comparable to values in the present. Can be either subjective or objective . |

Go to **Cram101.com** for the Practice Tests for this Chapter.

Conversion	Conversion refers to any distinct act of dominion wrongfully exerted over another's personal property in denial of or inconsistent with his rights therein. That tort committed by a person who deals with chattels not belonging to him in a manner that is inconsistent with the ownership of the lawful owner.
Frequency	Frequency refers to the speed of the up and down movements of a fluctuating economic variable; that is, the number of times per unit of time that the variable completes a cycle of up and down movement.
Annuities	Financial contracts under which a customer pays an annual premium in exchange for a future stream of annual payments beginning at a set age, say 65, and ending when the person dies are annuities.
Interest	In finance and economics, interest is the price paid by a borrower for the use of a lender's money. In other words, interest is the amount of paid to "rent" money for a period of time.
Annuity	A contract to make regular payments to a person for life or for a fixed period is an annuity.
Pension	A pension is a steady income given to a person (usually after retirement). Pensions are typically payments made in the form of a guaranteed annuity to a retired or disabled employee.
Fund	Independent accounting entity with a self-balancing set of accounts segregated for the purposes of carrying on specific activities is referred to as a fund.
Present value of an annuity	The sum of the present value of a series of consecutive equal payments is called present value of an annuity.
Present value	The value today of a stream of payments and/or receipts over time in the future and/or the past, converted to the present using an interest rate. If X t is the amount in period t and r the interest rate, then present value at time t=0 is V = ?T /t.
Argument	The discussion by counsel for the respective parties of their contentions on the law and the facts of the case being tried in order to aid the jury in arriving at a correct and just conclusion is called argument.
Consideration	Consideration in contract law, a basic requirement for an enforceable agreement under traditional contract principles, defined in this text as legal value, bargained for and given in exchange for an act or promise. In corporation law, cash or property contributed to a corporation in exchange for shares, or a promise to contribute such cash or property.
Perpetuity	A perpetuity is an annuity in which the periodic payments begin on a fixed date and continue indefinitely. Fixed coupon payments on permanently invested (irredeemable) sums of money are prime examples of perpetuities. Scholarships paid perpetually from an endowment fit the definition of perpetuity.
Investment	Investment refers to spending for the production and accumulation of capital and additions to inventories. In a financial sense, buying an asset with the expectation of making a return.
Interest rate	The rate of return on bonds, loans, or deposits. When one speaks of 'the' interest rate, it is usually in a model where there is only one.
Points	Loan origination fees that may be deductible as interest by a buyer of property. A seller of property who pays points reduces the selling price by the amount of the points paid for the buyer.
Integration	Economic integration refers to reducing barriers among countries to transactions and to movements of goods, capital, and labor, including harmonization of laws, regulations, and standards. Integrated markets theoretically function as a unified market.
Balance	In banking and accountancy, the outstanding balance is the amount of money owned, (or due),

that remains in a deposit account (or a loan account) at a given date, after all past remittances, payments and withdrawal have been accounted for. It can be positive (then, in the balance sheet of a firm, it is an asset) or negative (a liability).

Principal

In agency law, one under whose direction an agent acts and for whose benefit that agent acts is a principal.

Common stock

Common stock refers to the basic, normal, voting stock issued by a corporation; called residual equity because it ranks after preferred stock for dividend and liquidation distributions.

Variable

A variable is something measured by a number; it is used to analyze what happens to other things when the size of that number changes.

Stock

In financial terminology, stock is the capital raized by a corporation, through the issuance and sale of shares.

Nominal rate of interest

The nominal rate of interest is the percentage by which the money the borrower pays back exceeds the money that he borrowed, making no adjustment for any fall in the purchasing power of this money that results from inflation.

Simple interest

Simple interest is interest that accrues linearly. In other words, it grows by a certain fraction of the principal per time period.

18

Go to **Cram101.com** for the Practice Tests for this Chapter.

Discounted cash flow	In finance, the discounted cash flow approach describes a method to value a project or an entire company. The DCF methods determine the present value of future cash flows by discounting them using the appropriate cost of capital.
Cash flow	In finance, cash flow refers to the amounts of cash being received and spent by a business during a defined period of time, sometimes tied to a specific project. Most of the time they are being used to determine gaps in the liquid position of a company.
Yield	The interest rate that equates a future value or an annuity to a given present value is a yield.
Investment	Investment refers to spending for the production and accumulation of capital and additions to inventories. In a financial sense, buying an asset with the expectation of making a return.
Interest	In finance and economics, interest is the price paid by a borrower for the use of a lender's money. In other words, interest is the amount of paid to "rent" money for a period of time.
Fund	Independent accounting entity with a self-balancing set of accounts segregated for the purposes of carrying on specific activities is referred to as a fund.
Interest rate	The rate of return on bonds, loans, or deposits. When one speaks of 'the' interest rate, it is usually in a model where there is only one.
Financial transaction	A financial transaction involves a change in the status of the finances of two or more businesses or individuals.
Jurisdiction	The power of a court to hear and decide a case is called jurisdiction. It is the practical authority granted to a formally constituted body or to a person to deal with and make pronouncements on legal matters and, by implication, to administer justice within a defined area of responsibility.
Expense	In accounting, an expense represents an event in which an asset is used up or a liability is incurred. In terms of the accounting equation, expenses reduce owners' equity.
Contribution	In business organization law, the cash or property contributed to a business by its owners is referred to as contribution.
Present value	The value today of a stream of payments and/or receipts over time in the future and/or the past, converted to the present using an interest rate. If X t is the amount in period t and r the interest rate, then present value at time t=0 is V = ?T /t.
Internal rate of return	Internal rate of return refers to a discounted cash flow method for evaluating capital budgeting projects. The internal rate of return is a discount rate that makes the present value of the cash inflows equal to the present value of the cash outflows.
Rate of return	A rate of return is a comparison of the money earned (or lost) on an investment to the amount of money invested.
Lender	Suppliers and financial institutions that lend money to companies is referred to as a lender.
Return on investment	Return on investment refers to the return a businessperson gets on the money he and other owners invest in the firm; for example, a business that earned $100 on a $1,000 investment would have a ROI of 10 percent: 100 divided by 1000.
Comprehensive	A comprehensive refers to a layout accurate in size, color, scheme, and other necessary details to show how a final ad will look. For presentation only, never for reproduction.
Annuities	Financial contracts under which a customer pays an annual premium in exchange for a future stream of annual payments beginning at a set age, say 65, and ending when the person dies are annuities.
Annuity	A contract to make regular payments to a person for life or for a fixed period is an annuity.

Option	A contract that gives the purchaser the option to buy or sell the underlying financial instrument at a specified price, called the exercise price or strike price, within a specific period of time.
Remainder	A remainder in property law is a future interest created in a transferee that is capable of becoming possessory upon the natural termination of a prior estate created by the same instrument.
Balance	In banking and accountancy, the outstanding balance is the amount of money owned, (or due), that remains in a deposit account (or a loan account) at a given date, after all past remittances, payments and withdrawal have been accounted for. It can be positive (then, in the balance sheet of a firm, it is an asset) or negative (a liability).
Points	Loan origination fees that may be deductible as interest by a buyer of property. A seller of property who pays points reduces the selling price by the amount of the points paid for the buyer.
Consideration	Consideration in contract law, a basic requirement for an enforceable agreement under traditional contract principles, defined in this text as legal value, bargained for and given in exchange for an act or promise. In corporation law, cash or property contributed to a corporation in exchange for shares, or a promise to contribute such cash or property.
Reinvestment risk	Reinvestment risk describes the risk that a particular investment might be canceled or stopped somehow, that one may have to find a new place to invest that money with the risk being there might not be a similarly attractive investment available.
Principal	In agency law, one under whose direction an agent acts and for whose benefit that agent acts is a principal.
Compound interest	Compound interest is interest computed on the sum of all past interest added as well as on the principal.
Simple interest	Simple interest is interest that accrues linearly. In other words, it grows by a certain fraction of the principal per time period.
Insurance	Insurance refers to a system by which individuals can reduce their exposure to risk of large losses by spreading the risks among a large number of persons.
Asset	An item of property, such as land, capital, money, a share in ownership, or a claim on others for future payment, such as a bond or a bank deposit is an asset.
Accumulation	The acquisition of an increasing quantity of something. The accumulation of factors, especially capital, is a primary mechanism for economic growth.
Actual investment	Actual investment refers to the amount that firms do invest; equal to planned investment plus unplanned investment. Unplanned investment may be positive or negative.
Pro rata	Proportionate is referred to as pro rata. A method of equally and proportionately allocating money, profits or liabilities by percentage.
Portfolio	In finance, a portfolio is a collection of investments held by an institution or a private individual. Holding but not always a portfolio is part of an investment and risk-limiting strategy called diversification. By owning several assets, certain types of risk (in particular specific risk) can be reduced.
Capital	Capital generally refers to financial wealth, especially that used to start or maintain a business. In classical economics, capital is one of four factors of production, the others being land and labor and entrepreneurship.
Capital budgeting	Capital budgeting is the planning process used to determine a firm's long term investments such as new machinery, replacement machinery, new plants, new products, and research and

Go to **Cram101.com** for the Practice Tests for this Chapter.

	development projects.
Preference	The act of a debtor in paying or securing one or more of his creditors in a manner more favorable to them than to other creditors or to the exclusion of such other creditors is a preference. In the absence of statute, a preference is perfectly good, but to be legal it must be bona fide, and not a mere subterfuge of the debtor to secure a future benefit to himself or to prevent the application of his property to his debts.
Profit	Profit refers to the return to the resource entrepreneurial ability; total revenue minus total cost.
Net present value method	Capital budgeting DCF method that calculates the expected monetary gain or loss from a project by discounting all expected future cash inflows and outflows to the present point in time, using the required rate of return a net present value method.
Net present value	Net present value is a standard method in finance of capital budgeting – the planning of long-term investments. Using this method a potential investment project should be undertaken if the present value of all cash inflows minus the present value of all cash outflows (which equals the net present value) is greater than zero.
Argument	The discussion by counsel for the respective parties of their contentions on the law and the facts of the case being tried in order to aid the jury in arriving at a correct and just conclusion is called argument.
Cash outflow	Cash flowing out of the business from all sources over a period of time is cash outflow.
Cash inflow	Cash coming into the company as the result of a previous investment is a cash inflow.
Discount	The difference between the face value of a bond and its selling price, when a bond is sold for less than its face value it's referred to as a discount.
Exchange	The trade of things of value between buyer and seller so that each is better off after the trade is called the exchange.
Inception	The date and time on which coverage under an insurance policy takes effect is inception. Also refers to the date at which a stock or mutual fund was first traded.
Effective interest rate	Yield rate of bonds, which is usually equal to the market rate of interest on the day the bonds are sold is the effective interest rate.
Firm	An organization that employs resources to produce a good or service for profit and owns and operates one or more plants is referred to as a firm.
Variable	A variable is something measured by a number; it is used to analyze what happens to other things when the size of that number changes.
Policy	Similar to a script in that a policy can be a less than completely rational decision-making method. Involves the use of a pre-existing set of decision steps for any problem that presents itself.
Beneficiary	The person for whose benefit an insurance policy, trust, will, or contract is established is a beneficiary. In the case of a contract, the beneficiary is called a third-party beneficiary.
Credit	Credit refers to a recording as positive in the balance of payments, any transaction that gives rise to a payment into the country, such as an export, the sale of an asset, or borrowing from abroad.

Interest	In finance and economics, interest is the price paid by a borrower for the use of a lender's money. In other words, interest is the amount of paid to "rent" money for a period of time.
Extension	Extension refers to an out-of-court settlement in which creditors agree to allow the firm more time to meet its financial obligations. A new repayment schedule will be developed, subject to the acceptance of creditors.
Amortization schedule	An amortization schedule is a table detailing each periodic payment on a loan (typically a mortgage), as generated by an amortization calculator. They are calculated so that each periodic payment for the entirety of the loan is equal, making the repayment process somewhat simpler under amortization than with other models.
Amortization	Systematic and rational allocation of the acquisition cost of an intangible asset over its useful life is referred to as amortization.
Sinking fund	A sinking fund is a method by which an organization sets aside money over time to retire its indebtedness. More specifically, it is a fund into which money can be deposited, so that over time its preferred stock, debentures or stocks can be retired.
Balance	In banking and accountancy, the outstanding balance is the amount of money owned, (or due), that remains in a deposit account (or a loan account) at a given date, after all past remittances, payments and withdrawal have been accounted for. It can be positive (then, in the balance sheet of a firm, it is an asset) or negative (a liability).
Annuity	A contract to make regular payments to a person for life or for a fixed period is an annuity.
Fund	Independent accounting entity with a self-balancing set of accounts segregated for the purposes of carrying on specific activities is referred to as a fund.
Present value	The value today of a stream of payments and/or receipts over time in the future and/or the past, converted to the present using an interest rate. If X t is the amount in period t and r the interest rate, then present value at time t=0 is V = ?T /t.
Inception	The date and time on which coverage under an insurance policy takes effect is inception. Also refers to the date at which a stock or mutual fund was first traded.
Principal	In agency law, one under whose direction an agent acts and for whose benefit that agent acts is a principal.
Nominal rate of interest	The nominal rate of interest is the percentage by which the money the borrower pays back exceeds the money that he borrowed, making no adjustment for any fall in the purchasing power of this money that results from inflation.
Lender	Suppliers and financial institutions that lend money to companies is referred to as a lender.
Perpetuity	A perpetuity is an annuity in which the periodic payments begin on a fixed date and continue indefinitely. Fixed coupon payments on permanently invested (irredeemable) sums of money are prime examples of perpetuities. Scholarships paid perpetually from an endowment fit the definition of perpetuity.
Yield	The interest rate that equates a future value or an annuity to a given present value is a yield.
Net investment income	Net investment income refers to the interest and dividend income received by the residents of a nation from residents of other nations less the interest and dividend payments made by the residents of that nation to the residents of other nations.
Investment income	Investment income refers to consisting of virtually the same elements as portfolio income, a measure by which to justify a deduction for interest on investment indebtedness. Income derived from investments.

Investment	Investment refers to spending for the production and accumulation of capital and additions to inventories. In a financial sense, buying an asset with the expectation of making a return.
Net investment	In economics, net investment refers to an activity of spending which increases the availability of fixed capital goods or means of production. It is the total spending on new fixed investment minus replacement investment, which simply replaces depreciated capital goods.
Consideration	Consideration in contract law, a basic requirement for an enforceable agreement under traditional contract principles, defined in this text as legal value, bargained for and given in exchange for an act or promise. In corporation law, cash or property contributed to a corporation in exchange for shares, or a promise to contribute such cash or property.
Present value of an annuity	The sum of the present value of a series of consecutive equal payments is called present value of an annuity.
Holding	The holding is a court's determination of a matter of law based on the issue presented in the particular case. In other words: under this law, with these facts, this result.
Conversion	Conversion refers to any distinct act of dominion wrongfully exerted over another's personal property in denial of or inconsistent with his rights therein. That tort committed by a person who deals with chattels not belonging to him in a manner that is inconsistent with the ownership of the lawful owner.
Frequency	Frequency refers to the speed of the up and down movements of a fluctuating economic variable; that is, the number of times per unit of time that the variable completes a cycle of up and down movement.
Interest payment	The payment to holders of bonds payable, calculated by multiplying the stated rate on the face of the bond by the par, or face, value of the bond. If bonds are issued at a discount or premium, the interest payment does not equal the interest expense.
Amortization of loan	Systematic repayment of principal and interest over the life of a loan is an amortization of loan. While every payment is applied towards both the interest and the principal of the loan, the exact amount applied to principal each time (with the remainder going to interest) varies
Context	The effect of the background under which a message often takes on more and richer meaning is a context. Context is especially important in cross-cultural interactions because some cultures are said to be high context or low context.
Trial	An examination before a competent tribunal, according to the law of the land, of the facts or law put in issue in a cause, for the purpose of determining such issue is a trial. When the court hears and determines any issue of fact or law for the purpose of determining the rights of the parties, it may be considered a trial.
Amortize	To provide for the payment of a debt by creating a sinking fund or paying in installments is to amortize.
Mortgage	Mortgage refers to a note payable issued for property, such as a house, usually repaid in equal installments consisting of part principle and part interest, over a specified period.
Capital	Capital generally refers to financial wealth, especially that used to start or maintain a business. In classical economics, capital is one of four factors of production, the others being land and labor and entrepreneurship.
Accrued interest	In finance, accrued interest is the interest that has accumulated since the principal investment, or since the previous interest payment if there has been one already. For a financial instrument such as a bond, interest is calculated and paid in set intervals.
Accumulation	The acquisition of an increasing quantity of something. The accumulation of factors,

Go to Cram101.com for the Practice Tests for this Chapter.

especially capital, is a primary mechanism for economic growth.

Interest rate   The rate of return on bonds, loans, or deposits. When one speaks of 'the' interest rate, it is usually in a model where there is only one.

Insurance   Insurance refers to a system by which individuals can reduce their exposure to risk of large losses by spreading the risks among a large number of persons.

Security	Security refers to a claim on the borrower future income that is sold by the borrower to the lender. A security is a type of transferable interest representing financial value.
Market	A market is, as defined in economics, a social arrangement that allows buyers and sellers to discover information and carry out a voluntary exchange of goods or services.
Financial market	In economics, a financial market is a mechanism which allows people to trade money for securities or commodities such as gold or other precious metals. In general, any commodity market might be considered to be a financial market, if the usual purpose of traders is not the immediate consumption of the commodity, but rather as a means of delaying or accelerating consumption over time.
Financial instrument	Formal or legal documents in writing, such as contracts, deeds, wills, bonds, leases, and mortgages is referred to as a financial instrument.
Instrument	Instrument refers to an economic variable that is controlled by policy makers and can be used to influence other variables, called targets. Examples are monetary and fiscal policies used to achieve external and internal balance.
Corporation	A legal entity chartered by a state or the Federal government that is distinct and separate from the individuals who own it is a corporation. This separation gives the corporation unique powers which other legal entities lack.
Interest	In finance and economics, interest is the price paid by a borrower for the use of a lender's money. In other words, interest is the amount of paid to "rent" money for a period of time.
Capital	Capital generally refers to financial wealth, especially that used to start or maintain a business. In classical economics, capital is one of four factors of production, the others being land and labor and entrepreneurship.
Bond	Bond refers to a debt instrument, issued by a borrower and promising a specified stream of payments to the purchaser, usually regular interest payments plus a final repayment of principal.
Maturity	Maturity refers to the final payment date of a loan or other financial instrument, after which point no further interest or principal need be paid.
Maturity date	The date on which the final payment on a bond is due from the bond issuer to the investor is a maturity date.
Accumulation	The acquisition of an increasing quantity of something. The accumulation of factors, especially capital, is a primary mechanism for economic growth.
Coupon	In finance, a coupon is "attached" to a bond, either physically (as with old bonds) or electronically. Each coupon represents a predetermined payment promized to the bond-holder in return for his or her loan of money to the bond-issuer. .
Issuer	The company that borrows money from investors by issuing bonds is referred to as issuer. They are legally responsible for the obligations of the issue and for reporting financial conditions, material developments and any other operational activities as required by the regulations of their jurisdictions.
Coupon bond	A credit market instrument, the coupon bond pays the owner a fixed interest payment every year until the maturity date, when a specified final amount is repaid.
Zero coupon bond	A zero coupon bond is a bond which do not pay periodic coupons, or so-called "interest payments." They are purchased at a discount from their value at maturity. The holder of a zero coupon bond is entitled to receive a single payment, usually of a specified sum of money at a specified time in the future.
Unregistered	Unregistered bonds refer to coupon or bearer bonds; bonds for which no record of the holder

bonds	of the bond is kept.
Registered bond	A registered bond refers to a bond for which the issuing company keeps a record of the name and address of the bondholder and pays interest and principal payments directly to the registered owner.
Lender	Suppliers and financial institutions that lend money to companies is referred to as a lender.
Bearer bond	A bearer bond is a legal certificate that usually represents a bond obligation of, or stock in, a corporation or some other intangible property.
Possession	Possession refers to respecting real property, exclusive dominion and control such as owners of like property usually exercise over it. Manual control of personal property either as owner or as one having a qualified right in it.
Bearer	A person in possession of a negotiable instrument that is payable to him, his order, or to whoever is in possession of the instrument is referred to as bearer.
Holder	A person in possession of a document of title or an instrument payable or indorsed to him, his order, or to bearer is a holder.
Property	Assets defined in the broadest legal sense. Property includes the unrealized receivables of a cash basis taxpayer, but not services rendered.
Mortgage	Mortgage refers to a note payable issued for property, such as a house, usually repaid in equal installments consisting of part principle and part interest, over a specified period.
Mortgage bond	Type of secured bond that conditionally transfers title of a designated piece of property to the bondholder until the bond is paid is referred to as mortgage bond.
Real property	Real property is a legal term encompassing real estate and ownership interests in real estate (immovable property).
Debenture	A debenture is a long-term debt instrument used by governments and large companies to obtain funds. It is similar to a bond except the securitization conditions are different.
Credit	Credit refers to a recording as positive in the balance of payments, any transaction that gives rise to a payment into the country, such as an export, the sale of an asset, or borrowing from abroad.
Collateral	Property that is pledged to the lender to guarantee payment in the event that the borrower is unable to make debt payments is called collateral.
Default	In finance, default occurs when a debtor has not met its legal obligations according to the debt contract, e.g. it has not made a scheduled payment, or violated a covenant (condition) of the debt contract.
Investment	Investment refers to spending for the production and accumulation of capital and additions to inventories. In a financial sense, buying an asset with the expectation of making a return.
Convertible bond	A convertible bond is type of bond that can be converted into shares of stock in the issuing company, usually at some pre-announced ratio.
Fund	Independent accounting entity with a self-balancing set of accounts segregated for the purposes of carrying on specific activities is referred to as a fund.
Treasury bills	Short-term obligations of the federal government are treasury bills. They are like zero coupon bonds in that they do not pay interest prior to maturity; instead they are sold at a discount of the par value to create a positive yield to maturity.
Treasury notes	Intermediate-term obligations of the federal government with maturities from 1 to 10 years are called treasury notes.

Treasury security	A treasury security is a government bond issued by the United States Department of the Treasury through the Bureau of the Public Debt. They are the debt financing instruments of the U.S. Federal government, and are often referred to simply as Treasuries.
Creditor	A person to whom a debt or legal obligation is owed, and who has the right to enforce payment of that debt or obligation is referred to as creditor.
Stock	In financial terminology, stock is the capital raized by a corporation, through the issuance and sale of shares.
Preferred stock	Stock that has specified rights over common stock is a preferred stock.
Dividend	Amount of corporate profits paid out for each share of stock is referred to as dividend.
Cumulative preferred stock	Cumulative preferred stock is preferred stock whose dividends accumulate unpaid until paid out, there by allowing companies to postpone dividend payments.
Common stock	Common stock refers to the basic, normal, voting stock issued by a corporation; called residual equity because it ranks after preferred stock for dividend and liquidation distributions.
A share	In finance the term A share has two distinct meanings, both relating to securities. The first is a designation for a 'class' of common or preferred stock. A share of common or preferred stock typically has enhanced voting rights or other benefits compared to the other forms of shares that may have been created. The equity structure, or how many types of shares are offered, is determined by the corporate charter.
Participating Preferred Stock	Participating preferred stock refers to a small number of preferred stock issues are participating with regard to corporate earnings. For such issues, once the common stock dividend equals the preferred stock dividend, the two classes of securities may share equally in additional dividend payments.
Convertible preferred stock	Preferred stock that includes an option for the holder to convert the preferred shares into a fixed number of common shares, usually anytime after a predetermined date is convertible preferred stock.
Privilege	Generally, a legal right to engage in conduct that would otherwise result in legal liability is a privilege. Privileges are commonly classified as absolute or conditional. Occasionally, privilege is also used to denote a legal right to refrain from particular behavior.
Option	A contract that gives the purchaser the option to buy or sell the underlying financial instrument at a specified price, called the exercise price or strike price, within a specific period of time.
Interest payment	The payment to holders of bonds payable, calculated by multiplying the stated rate on the face of the bond by the par, or face, value of the bond. If bonds are issued at a discount or premium, the interest payment does not equal the interest expense.
Stock dividend	Stock dividend refers to pro rata distributions of stock or stock rights on common stock. They are usually issued in proportion to shares owned.
Board of directors	The group of individuals elected by the stockholders of a corporation to oversee its operations is a board of directors.
Variable	A variable is something measured by a number; it is used to analyze what happens to other things when the size of that number changes.
Yield	The interest rate that equates a future value or an annuity to a given present value is a yield.
Discount	The difference between the face value of a bond and its selling price, when a bond is sold

Go to **Cram101.com** for the Practice Tests for this Chapter.

for less than its face value it's referred to as a discount.

Callable bond A callable bond is a bond that can be redeemed by the issuer prior to its maturity, on certain dates, at a price determined at issuance.

Par value The central value of a pegged exchange rate, around which the actual rate is permitted to fluctuate within set bounds is a par value.

At par At equality refers to at par. Two currencies are said to be 'at par' if they are trading one-for-one.

Frequency Frequency refers to the speed of the up and down movements of a fluctuating economic variable; that is, the number of times per unit of time that the variable completes a cycle of up and down movement.

Yield to maturity Yield to maturity refers to the required rate of return on a bond issue. It is the discount rate used in present-valuing future interest payments and the principal payment at maturity. The term is used interchangeably with market rate of interest.

Interest rate The rate of return on bonds, loans, or deposits. When one speaks of 'the' interest rate, it is usually in a model where there is only one.

Internal rate of return Internal rate of return refers to a discounted cash flow method for evaluating capital budgeting projects. The internal rate of return is a discount rate that makes the present value of the cash inflows equal to the present value of the cash outflows.

Coupon rate In bonds, notes or other fixed income securities, the stated percentage rate of interest, usually paid twice a year is the coupon rate.

Rate of return A rate of return is a comparison of the money earned (or lost) on an investment to the amount of money invested.

Conversion Conversion refers to any distinct act of dominion wrongfully exerted over another's personal property in denial of or inconsistent with his rights therein. That tort committed by a person who deals with chattels not belonging to him in a manner that is inconsistent with the ownership of the lawful owner.

Current yield Current yield refers to the rate of return on a bond; the annual interest payment divided by the bond's price.

Inverse relationship The relationship between two variables that change in opposite directions, for example, product price and quantity demanded is an inverse relationship.

Present value The value today of a stream of payments and/or receipts over time in the future and/or the past, converted to the present using an interest rate. If X_t is the amount in period t and r the interest rate, then present value at time t=0 is $V = ?T /t$.

Premium Premium refers to the fee charged by an insurance company for an insurance policy. The rate of losses must be relatively predictable: In order to set the premium (prices) insurers must be able to estimate them accurately.

Profit Profit refers to the return to the resource entrepreneurial ability; total revenue minus total cost.

Principal In agency law, one under whose direction an agent acts and for whose benefit that agent acts is a principal.

Financial statement Financial statement refers to a summary of all the transactions that have occurred over a particular period.

Pension fund Amounts of money put aside by corporations, nonprofit organizations, or unions to cover part of the financial needs of members when they retire is a pension fund.

Book value	The book value of an asset or group of assets is sometimes the price at which they were originally acquired, in many cases equal to purchase price.
Insurance	Insurance refers to a system by which individuals can reduce their exposure to risk of large losses by spreading the risks among a large number of persons.
Pension	A pension is a steady income given to a person (usually after retirement). Pensions are typically payments made in the form of a guaranteed annuity to a retired or disabled employee.
Asset	An item of property, such as land, capital, money, a share in ownership, or a claim on others for future payment, such as a bond or a bank deposit is an asset.
Balance	In banking and accountancy, the outstanding balance is the amount of money owned, (or due), that remains in a deposit account (or a loan account) at a given date, after all past remittances, payments and withdrawal have been accounted for. It can be positive (then, in the balance sheet of a firm, it is an asset) or negative (a liability).
Amortization	Systematic and rational allocation of the acquisition cost of an intangible asset over its useful life is referred to as amortization.
Market price	Market price is an economic concept with commonplace familiarity; it is the price that a good or service is offered at, or will fetch, in the marketplace; it is of interest mainly in the study of microeconomics.
Sinking fund	A sinking fund is a method by which an organization sets aside money over time to retire its indebtedness. More specifically, it is a fund into which money can be deposited, so that over time its preferred stock, debentures or stocks can be retired.
Premium Bond	A Premium Bond is a bond issued by the United Kingdom government's National Savings and Investments scheme. The government promises to buy back the bond on request for its original price.
Discount bond	Discount bond refers to a credit market instrument that is bought at a price below its face value and whose face value is repaid at the maturity date; it does not make any interest payments.
Book value of a bond	Book value of a bond refers to bonds payable plus the unamortized premium or the bonds payable minus the unamortized discount; also known as the carrying value of a bond.
Valuation	In finance, valuation is the process of estimating the market value of a financial asset or liability. They can be done on assets (for example, investments in marketable securities such as stocks, options, business enterprises, or intangible assets such as patents and trademarks) or on liabilities (e.g., Bonds issued by a company).
Points	Loan origination fees that may be deductible as interest by a buyer of property. A seller of property who pays points reduces the selling price by the amount of the points paid for the buyer.
Market value	Market value refers to the price of an asset agreed on between a willing buyer and a willing seller; the price an asset could demand if it is sold on the open market.
Compound interest	Compound interest is interest computed on the sum of all past interest added as well as on the principal.
Simple interest	Simple interest is interest that accrues linearly. In other words, it grows by a certain fraction of the principal per time period.
Pro rata	Proportionate is referred to as pro rata. A method of equally and proportionately allocating money, profits or liabilities by percentage.

Go to **Cram101.com** for the Practice Tests for this Chapter.

Industry	A group of firms that produce identical or similar products is an industry. It is also used specifically to refer to an area of economic production focused on manufacturing which involves large amounts of capital investment before any profit can be realized, also called "heavy industry".
Convergence	The blending of various facets of marketing functions and communication technology to create more efficient and expanded synergies is a convergence.
Ad hoc	Ad hoc is a Latin phrase which means "for this purpose." It generally signifies a solution that has been tailored to a specific purpose and is makeshift and non-general, such as a handcrafted network protocol or a specific-purpose equation, as opposed to general solutions.
Consideration	Consideration in contract law, a basic requirement for an enforceable agreement under traditional contract principles, defined in this text as legal value, bargained for and given in exchange for an act or promise. In corporation law, cash or property contributed to a corporation in exchange for shares, or a promise to contribute such cash or property.
Expense	In accounting, an expense represents an event in which an asset is used up or a liability is incurred. In terms of the accounting equation, expenses reduce owners' equity.
Gain	In finance, gain is a profit or an increase in value of an investment such as a stock or bond. Gain is calculated by fair market value or the proceeds from the sale of the investment minus the sum of the purchase price and all costs associated with it.
Trial	An examination before a competent tribunal, according to the law of the land, of the facts or law put in issue in a cause, for the purpose of determining such issue is a trial. When the court hears and determines any issue of fact or law for the purpose of determining the rights of the parties, it may be considered a trial.
Serial bonds	Serial bonds refer to bonds in an issue that mature periodically over several years, usually at varying interest rates.
Annuity	A contract to make regular payments to a person for life or for a fixed period is an annuity.
Redeemable bond	A bonds that can be redeemed or paid off by the issuer prior to the bonds' maturity date is called a redeemable bond.
Perpetual bond	A perpetual bond is a bond with no maturity date. Perpetual bonds pay coupons forever, and the issuer does not have to redeem them. Their cash flows are therefore that of a perpetuity.
Stock market	An organized marketplace in which common stocks are traded. In the United States, the largest stock market is the New York Stock Exchange, on which are traded the stocks of the largest U.S. companies.
Institutional investors	Institutional investors refers to large organizations such as pension funds, mutual funds, insurance companies, and banks that invest their own funds or the funds of others.
Accounting	A system that collects and processes financial information about an organization and reports that information to decision makers is referred to as accounting.
Unrealized capital gain	Unrealized capital gain occurs when it is known that the asset has appreciated in value, but the asset has not been sold yet; the gain is only potential.
Capital loss	Capital loss refers to the loss in value that the owner of an asset experiences when the price of the asset falls, including when the currency in which the asset is denominated depreciates. Contrasts with capital gain.
Capital gain	Capital gain refers to the gain in value that the owner of an asset experiences when the price of the asset rises, including when the currency in which the asset is denominated appreciates.

Realized capital gain	A capital gain that is obtained when a stock is sold for a higher price than the price paid for it is a realized capital gain.
Portfolio	In finance, a portfolio is a collection of investments held by an institution or a private individual. Holding but not always a portfolio is part of an investment and risk-limiting strategy called diversification. By owning several assets, certain types of risk (in particular specific risk) can be reduced.
Compounded semiannually	A compounding period of every six months is called compounded semiannually.
Discount rate	Discount rate refers to the rate, per year, at which future values are diminished to make them comparable to values in the present. Can be either subjective or objective .
Amortization schedule	An amortization schedule is a table detailing each periodic payment on a loan (typically a mortgage), as generated by an amortization calculator. They are calculated so that each periodic payment for the entirety of the loan is equal, making the repayment process somewhat simpler under amortization than with other models.
Purchasing	Purchasing refers to the function in a firm that searches for quality material resources, finds the best suppliers, and negotiates the best price for goods and services.
Buyer	A buyer refers to a role in the buying center with formal authority and responsibility to select the supplier and negotiate the terms of the contract.
Date of issue	As applied to notes, bonds, and so on of a series, the arbitrary date fixed as the beginning of the term for which they run, without reference to the precise time when convenience or the state of the market may permit their sale or delivery is called the date of issue.
Earnings per share	Earnings per share refers to annual profit of the corporation divided by the number of shares outstanding.
Corporate bond	A Corporate bond is a bond issued by a corporation, as the name suggests. The term is usually applied to longer term debt instruments, generally with a maturity date falling at least 12 months after their issue date (the term "commercial paper" being sometimes used for instruments with a shorter maturity).
Shares	Shares refer to an equity security, representing a shareholder's ownership of a corporation. Shares are one of a finite number of equal portions in the capital of a company, entitling the owner to a proportion of distributed, non-reinvested profits known as dividends and to a portion of the value of the company in case of liquidation.

Credit	Credit refers to a recording as positive in the balance of payments, any transaction that gives rise to a payment into the country, such as an export, the sale of an asset, or borrowing from abroad.
Financial analysis	Financial analysis is the analysis of the accounts and the economic prospects of a firm.
Investment	Investment refers to spending for the production and accumulation of capital and additions to inventories. In a financial sense, buying an asset with the expectation of making a return.
Fixed asset	Fixed asset, also known as property, plant, and equipment (PP&E), is a term used in accountancy for assets and property which cannot easily be converted into cash. This can be compared with current assets such as cash or bank accounts, which are described as liquid assets. In most cases, only tangible assets are referred to as fixed.
Asset	An item of property, such as land, capital, money, a share in ownership, or a claim on others for future payment, such as a bond or a bank deposit is an asset.
Lender	Suppliers and financial institutions that lend money to companies is referred to as a lender.
Disclosure	Disclosure means the giving out of information, either voluntarily or to be in compliance with legal regulations or workplace rules.
Annual percentage rate	Annual percentage rate refers to a measure of the effective rate on a loan. One uses the actuarial method of compound interest when calculating the annual percentage rate.
Interest	In finance and economics, interest is the price paid by a borrower for the use of a lender's money. In other words, interest is the amount of paid to "rent" money for a period of time.
Regulation	Regulation refers to restrictions state and federal laws place on business with regard to the conduct of its activities.
Federal Reserve	The Federal Reserve System was created via the Federal Reserve Act of December 23rd, 1913. All national banks were required to join the system and other banks could join. The Reserve Banks opened for business on November 16th, 1914. Federal Reserve Notes were created as part of the legislation, to provide an elastic supply of currency.
Balance	In banking and accountancy, the outstanding balance is the amount of money owned, (or due), that remains in a deposit account (or a loan account) at a given date, after all past remittances, payments and withdrawal have been accounted for. It can be positive (then, in the balance sheet of a firm, it is an asset) or negative (a liability).
Present value	The value today of a stream of payments and/or receipts over time in the future and/or the past, converted to the present using an interest rate. If X t is the amount in period t and r the interest rate, then present value at time t=0 is V = ?T /t.
Points	Loan origination fees that may be deductible as interest by a buyer of property. A seller of property who pays points reduces the selling price by the amount of the points paid for the buyer.
Yield	The interest rate that equates a future value or an annuity to a given present value is a yield.
Inception	The date and time on which coverage under an insurance policy takes effect is inception. Also refers to the date at which a stock or mutual fund was first traded.
Interest rate	The rate of return on bonds, loans, or deposits. When one speaks of 'the' interest rate, it is usually in a model where there is only one.
Merchant	Under the Uniform Commercial Code, one who regularly deals in goods of the kind sold in the contract at issue, or holds himself out as having special knowledge or skill relevant to such

goods, or who makes the sale through an agent who regularly deals in such goods or claims such knowledge or skill is referred to as merchant.

Simple interest	Simple interest is interest that accrues linearly. In other words, it grows by a certain fraction of the principal per time period.
Creditor	A person to whom a debt or legal obligation is owed, and who has the right to enforce payment of that debt or obligation is referred to as creditor.
Accrued interest	In finance, accrued interest is the interest that has accumulated since the principal investment, or since the previous interest payment if there has been one already. For a financial instrument such as a bond, interest is calculated and paid in set intervals.
Principal	In agency law, one under whose direction an agent acts and for whose benefit that agent acts is a principal.
Frequency	Frequency refers to the speed of the up and down movements of a fluctuating economic variable; that is, the number of times per unit of time that the variable completes a cycle of up and down movement.
Dealer	People who link buyers with sellers by buying and selling securities at stated prices are referred to as a dealer.
Option	A contract that gives the purchaser the option to buy or sell the underlying financial instrument at a specified price, called the exercise price or strike price, within a specific period of time.
Conversion	Conversion refers to any distinct act of dominion wrongfully exerted over another's personal property in denial of or inconsistent with his rights therein. That tort committed by a person who deals with chattels not belonging to him in a manner that is inconsistent with the ownership of the lawful owner.
Mortgage	Mortgage refers to a note payable issued for property, such as a house, usually repaid in equal installments consisting of part principle and part interest, over a specified period.
Estate	An estate is the totality of the legal rights, interests, entitlements and obligations attaching to property. In the context of wills and probate, it refers to the totality of the property which the deceased owned or in which some interest was held.
Buyer	A buyer refers to a role in the buying center with formal authority and responsibility to select the supplier and negotiate the terms of the contract.
Expense	In accounting, an expense represents an event in which an asset is used up or a liability is incurred. In terms of the accounting equation, expenses reduce owners' equity.
Preparation	Preparation refers to usually the first stage in the creative process. It includes education and formal training.
Credit report	Information about a person's credit history that can be secured from a credit bureau is referred to as credit report.
Amortization schedule	An amortization schedule is a table detailing each periodic payment on a loan (typically a mortgage), as generated by an amortization calculator. They are calculated so that each periodic payment for the entirety of the loan is equal, making the repayment process somewhat simpler under amortization than with other models.
Amortization	Systematic and rational allocation of the acquisition cost of an intangible asset over its useful life is referred to as amortization.
Portfolio	In finance, a portfolio is a collection of investments held by an institution or a private individual. Holding but not always a portfolio is part of an investment and risk-limiting

strategy called diversification. By owning several assets, certain types of risk (in particular specific risk) can be reduced.

Market	A market is, as defined in economics, a social arrangement that allows buyers and sellers to discover information and carry out a voluntary exchange of goods or services.
Margin	A deposit by a buyer in stocks with a seller or a stockbroker, as security to cover fluctuations in the market in reference to stocks that the buyer has purchased but for which he has not paid is a margin. Commodities are also traded on margin.
Firm	An organization that employs resources to produce a good or service for profit and owns and operates one or more plants is referred to as a firm.
Mortgage company	Mortgage company refers to a financial institution that lends money to borrowers to purchase property.
Appeal	Appeal refers to the act of asking an appellate court to overturn a decision after the trial court's final judgment has been entered.
Appreciation	Appreciation refers to a rise in the value of a country's currency on the exchange market, relative either to a particular other currency or to a weighted average of other currencies. The currency is said to appreciate. Opposite of 'depreciation.' Appreciation can also refer to the increase in value of any asset.
Exchange	The trade of things of value between buyer and seller so that each is better off after the trade is called the exchange.
Property	Assets defined in the broadest legal sense. Property includes the unrealized receivables of a cash basis taxpayer, but not services rendered.
Total cost	The sum of fixed cost and variable cost is referred to as total cost.
Annuity	A contract to make regular payments to a person for life or for a fixed period is an annuity.
Equity	Equity is the name given to the set of legal principles, in countries following the English common law tradition, which supplement strict rules of law where their application would operate harshly, so as to achieve what is sometimes referred to as "natural justice."
Compound interest	Compound interest is interest computed on the sum of all past interest added as well as on the principal.
Installment loan	A borrowing arrangement in which a schedule of equal payments are used to pay off a loan is called installment loan.
Argument	The discussion by counsel for the respective parties of their contentions on the law and the facts of the case being tried in order to aid the jury in arriving at a correct and just conclusion is called argument.
Annuities	Financial contracts under which a customer pays an annual premium in exchange for a future stream of annual payments beginning at a set age, say 65, and ending when the person dies are annuities.
Depreciation	Depreciation is an accounting and finance term for the method of attributing the cost of an asset across the useful life of the asset. Depreciation is a reduction in the value of a currency in floating exchange rate.
Accounting	A system that collects and processes financial information about an organization and reports that information to decision makers is referred to as accounting.
Book value	The book value of an asset or group of assets is sometimes the price at which they were originally acquired, in many cases equal to purchase price.

Go to **Cram101.com** for the Practice Tests for this Chapter.

Consideration	Consideration in contract law, a basic requirement for an enforceable agreement under traditional contract principles, defined in this text as legal value, bargained for and given in exchange for an act or promise. In corporation law, cash or property contributed to a corporation in exchange for shares, or a promise to contribute such cash or property.
Deductible	The dollar sum of costs that an insured individual must pay before the insurer begins to pay is called deductible.
Sinking fund	A sinking fund is a method by which an organization sets aside money over time to retire its indebtedness. More specifically, it is a fund into which money can be deposited, so that over time its preferred stock, debentures or stocks can be retired.
Fund	Independent accounting entity with a self-balancing set of accounts segregated for the purposes of carrying on specific activities is referred to as a fund.
Capital	Capital generally refers to financial wealth, especially that used to start or maintain a business. In classical economics, capital is one of four factors of production, the others being land and labor and entrepreneurship.
Discount	The difference between the face value of a bond and its selling price, when a bond is sold for less than its face value it's referred to as a discount.
Supply	Supply is the aggregate amount of any material good that can be called into being at a certain price point; it comprises one half of the equation of supply and demand. In classical economic theory, a curve representing supply is one of the factors that produce price.
Salvage value	In accounting, the salvage value of an asset is its remaining value after depreciation. The estimated value of an asset at the end of its useful life.
Confirmed	When the seller's bank agrees to assume liability on the letter of credit issued by the buyer's bank the transaction is confirmed.The term means that the credit is not only backed up by the issuing foreign bank, but that payment is also guaranteed by the notifying American bank.
Depreciation expense	Depreciation expense refers to the amount recognized as an expense in one period resulting from the periodic recognition of the used portion of the cost of a long-term tangible asset over its life.
Perpetuity	A perpetuity is an annuity in which the periodic payments begin on a fixed date and continue indefinitely. Fixed coupon payments on permanently invested (irredeemable) sums of money are prime examples of perpetuities. Scholarships paid perpetually from an endowment fit the definition of perpetuity.
Operation	A standardized method or technique that is performed repetitively, often on different materials resulting in different finished goods is called an operation.
Inflation	An increase in the overall price level of an economy, usually as measured by the CPI or by the implicit price deflator is called inflation.
Short sale	The sale of an asset the seller doesn't own at the time of the sale in the hope of purchasing the asset profitably at a lower price in the future to make the promized delivery is a short sale.
Security	Security refers to a claim on the borrower future income that is sold by the borrower to the lender. A security is a type of transferable interest representing financial value.
Context	The effect of the background under which a message often takes on more and richer meaning is a context. Context is especially important in cross-cultural interactions because some cultures are said to be high context or low context.
Profit	Profit refers to the return to the resource entrepreneurial ability; total revenue minus

total cost.

Short position	In finance, a short position in a security, such as a stock or a Bond, means the holder of the position has sold a security that he does not own, with the intention to buy it back at a later time at a lower price.
Residual	Residual payments can refer to an ongoing stream of payments in respect of the completion of past achievements.
Short selling	Short selling refers to when an investor places a speculative bet that the value of a financial asset will decline, and profits from that decline.
Dividend	Amount of corporate profits paid out for each share of stock is referred to as dividend.
Bond	Bond refers to a debt instrument, issued by a borrower and promising a specified stream of payments to the purchaser, usually regular interest payments plus a final repayment of principal.
Brief	Brief refers to a statement of a party's case or legal arguments, usually prepared by an attorney. Also used to make legal arguments before appellate courts.
Hedging	A technique for avoiding a risk by making a counteracting transaction is referred to as hedging.
Market price	Market price is an economic concept with commonplace familiarity; it is the price that a good or service is offered at, or will fetch, in the marketplace; it is of interest mainly in the study of microeconomics.
Arbitrage	An arbitrage is a combination of nearly simultaneous transactions designed to profit from an existing discrepancy among prices, exchange rates, and/or interest rates on different markets without assuming risk.
Common stock	Common stock refers to the basic, normal, voting stock issued by a corporation; called residual equity because it ranks after preferred stock for dividend and liquidation distributions.
Stock	In financial terminology, stock is the capital raized by a corporation, through the issuance and sale of shares.
Preferred stock	Stock that has specified rights over common stock is a preferred stock.
Callable bond	A callable bond is a bond that can be redeemed by the issuer prior to its maturity, on certain dates, at a price determined at issuance.
Convertible bond	A convertible bond is type of bond that can be converted into shares of stock in the issuing company, usually at some pre-announced ratio.
Issuer	The company that borrows money from investors by issuing bonds is referred to as issuer. They are legally responsible for the obligations of the issue and for reporting financial conditions, material developments and any other operational activities as required by the regulations of their jurisdictions.
Holder	A person in possession of a document of title or an instrument payable or indorsed to him, his order, or to bearer is a holder.
Money market	The money market, in macroeconomics and international finance, refers to the equilibration of demand for a country's domestic money to its money supply; market for short-term financial instruments.
Liquidity	Liquidity refers to the capacity to turn assets into cash, or the amount of assets in a portfolio that have that capacity.

Go to **Cram101.com** for the Practice Tests for this Chapter.

Instrument	Instrument refers to an economic variable that is controlled by policy makers and can be used to influence other variables, called targets. Examples are monetary and fiscal policies used to achieve external and internal balance.
Private sector	The households and business firms of the economy are referred to as private sector.
Certificates of deposit	Certificates of deposit refer to a certificate offered by banks, savings and loans, and other financial institutions for the deposit of funds at a given interest rate over a specified time period.
Variable	A variable is something measured by a number; it is used to analyze what happens to other things when the size of that number changes.
Secondary market	Secondary market refers to the market for securities that have already been issued. It is a market in which investors trade back and forth with each other.
Maturity	Maturity refers to the final payment date of a loan or other financial instrument, after which point no further interest or principal need be paid.
Pension fund	Amounts of money put aside by corporations, nonprofit organizations, or unions to cover part of the financial needs of members when they retire is a pension fund.
Insurance	Insurance refers to a system by which individuals can reduce their exposure to risk of large losses by spreading the risks among a large number of persons.
Contract	A contract is a "promise" or an "agreement" that is enforced or recognized by the law. In the civil law, a contract is considered to be part of the general law of obligations.
Pension	A pension is a steady income given to a person (usually after retirement). Pensions are typically payments made in the form of a guaranteed annuity to a retired or disabled employee.
Treasury security	A treasury security is a government bond issued by the United States Department of the Treasury through the Bureau of the Public Debt. They are the debt financing instruments of the U.S. Federal government, and are often referred to simply as Treasuries.
Matching	Matching refers to an accounting concept that establishes when expenses are recognized. Expenses are matched with the revenues they helped to generate and are recognized when those revenues are recognized.
Mutual fund	A mutual fund is a form of collective investment that pools money from many investors and invests the money in stocks, bonds, short-term money market instruments, and/or other securities. In a mutual fund, the fund manager trades the fund's underlying securities, realizing capital gains or loss, and collects the dividend or interest income.
Corporation	A legal entity chartered by a state or the Federal government that is distinct and separate from the individuals who own it is a corporation. This separation gives the corporation unique powers which other legal entities lack.
Federal National Mortgage Association	Federal National Mortgage Association refers to a former government agency that provides a secondary market in mortgages. It is now private.It is a United States Government-sponsored corporation created in 1938 to establish a secondary market for mortgages insured by the Federal Housing Administration (FHA).
Collateralized mortgage obligation	A collateralized mortgage obligation, created in June 1983 by investment banks Salomon Brothers and First Boston, is a type of mortgage-backed security, which has been divided up into tranches.
Financial instrument	Formal or legal documents in writing, such as contracts, deeds, wills, bonds, leases, and mortgages is referred to as a financial instrument.

Go to **Cram101.com** for the Practice Tests for this Chapter.

Cash flow	In finance, cash flow refers to the amounts of cash being received and spent by a business during a defined period of time, sometimes tied to a specific project. Most of the time they are being used to determine gaps in the liquid position of a company.
Maturity date	The date on which the final payment on a bond is due from the bond issuer to the investor is a maturity date.
Reinvestment risk	Reinvestment risk describes the risk that a particular investment might be canceled or stopped somehow, that one may have to find a new place to invest that money with the risk being there might not be a similarly attractive investment available.
Corporate bond	A Corporate bond is a bond issued by a corporation, as the name suggests. The term is usually applied to longer term debt instruments, generally with a maturity date falling at least 12 months after their issue date (the term "commercial paper" being sometimes used for instruments with a shorter maturity).
Fixed price	Fixed price is a phrase used to mean that no bargaining is allowed over the price of a good or, less commonly, a service.
Exercise price	Exercise price refers to the price at which the purchaser of an option has the right to buy or sell the underlying financial instrument. Also known as the strike price.
European option	An option that can be exercized only at the expiration date of the contract is referred to as european option.
American option	A stock option that can be exercized at any time up to the expiration date of the contract is referred to as American option.
Future interest	Future interest refers to an interest that will come into being at some future time. It is distinguished from a present interest, which already exists. Assume that Dan transfers securities to a newly created trust.
Warrant	A warrant is a security that entitles the holder to buy or sell a certain additional quantity of an underlying security at an agreed-upon price, at the holder's discretion.
Futures	Futures refer to contracts for the sale and future delivery of stocks or commodities, wherein either party may waive delivery, and receive or pay, as the case may be, the difference in market price at the time set for delivery.
Futures contract	In finance, a futures contract is a standardized contract, traded on a futures exchange, to buy or sell a certain underlying instrument at a certain date in the future, at a pre-set price. The
Open market	In economics, the open market is the term used to refer to the environment in which bonds are bought and sold.
Swap	In finance a swap is a derivative, where two counterparties exchange one stream of cash flows against another stream. These streams are called the legs of the swap. The cash flows are calculated over a notional principal amount. Swaps are often used to hedge certain risks, for instance interest rate risk. Another use is speculation.
Exchange rate	Exchange rate refers to the price at which one country's currency trades for another, typically on the exchange market.
Remainder	A remainder in property law is a future interest created in a transferee that is capable of becoming possessory upon the natural termination of a prior estate created by the same instrument.
Financial market	In economics, a financial market is a mechanism which allows people to trade money for securities or commodities such as gold or other precious metals. In general, any commodity market might be considered to be a financial market, if the usual purpose of traders is not

the immediate consumption of the commodity, but rather as a means of delaying or accelerating consumption over time.

Line of credit

Line of credit refers to a given amount of unsecured short-term funds a bank will lend to a business, provided the funds are readily available.

Closing

The finalization of a real estate sales transaction that passes title to the property from the seller to the buyer is referred to as a closing. Closing is a sales term which refers to the process of making a sale. It refers to reaching the final step, which may be an exchange of money or acquiring a signature.

Effective interest rate

Yield rate of bonds, which is usually equal to the market rate of interest on the day the bonds are sold is the effective interest rate.

Purchasing

Purchasing refers to the function in a firm that searches for quality material resources, finds the best suppliers, and negotiates the best price for goods and services.

Useful life

The length of service of a productive facility or piece of equipment is its useful life. The period of time during which an asset will have economic value and be usable.

Go to **Cram101.com** for the Practice Tests for this Chapter.

Present value	The value today of a stream of payments and/or receipts over time in the future and/or the past, converted to the present using an interest rate. If X t is the amount in period t and r the interest rate, then present value at time t=0 is $V = ?T /t$.
Financial analysis	Financial analysis is the analysis of the accounts and the economic prospects of a firm.
Interest	In finance and economics, interest is the price paid by a borrower for the use of a lender's money. In other words, interest is the amount of paid to "rent" money for a period of time.
Interest rate	The rate of return on bonds, loans, or deposits. When one speaks of 'the' interest rate, it is usually in a model where there is only one.
Market	A market is, as defined in economics, a social arrangement that allows buyers and sellers to discover information and carry out a voluntary exchange of goods or services.
Liability	A liability is a present obligation of the enterprise arizing from past events, the settlement of which is expected to result in an outflow from the enterprise of resources embodying economic benefits.
Asset	An item of property, such as land, capital, money, a share in ownership, or a claim on others for future payment, such as a bond or a bank deposit is an asset.
Lender	Suppliers and financial institutions that lend money to companies is referred to as a lender.
Economy	The income, expenditures, and resources that affect the cost of running a business and household are called an economy.
Usury	Usury refers to the taking of more than the law allows on a loan or for forbearance of a debt. Illegal interest.
Karl Marx	Karl Marx (May 5, 1818, Trier, Germany – March 14, 1883, London) was an immensely influential German philosopher, political economist, and socialist revolutionary. He is most famous for his analysis of history in terms of class struggles, summed up in the opening line of the introduction to the Communist Manifesto: "The history of all hitherto existing society is the history of class struggles."
Wage	The payment for the service of a unit of labor, per unit time. In trade theory, it is the only payment to labor, usually unskilled labor. In empirical work, wage data may exclude other compenzation, which must be added to get the total cost of employment.
Capital	Capital generally refers to financial wealth, especially that used to start or maintain a business. In classical economics, capital is one of four factors of production, the others being land and labor and entrepreneurship.
Preference	The act of a debtor in paying or securing one or more of his creditors in a manner more favorable to them than to other creditors or to the exclusion of such other creditors is a preference. In the absence of statute, a preference is perfectly good, but to be legal it must be bona fide, and not a mere subterfuge of the debtor to secure a future benefit to himself or to prevent the application of his property to his debts.
Supply	Supply is the aggregate amount of any material good that can be called into being at a certain price point; it comprises one half of the equation of supply and demand. In classical economic theory, a curve representing supply is one of the factors that produce price.
Firm	An organization that employs resources to produce a good or service for profit and owns and operates one or more plants is referred to as a firm.
Productivity	Productivity refers to the total output of goods and services in a given period of time divided by work hours.

Go to **Cram101.com** for the Practice Tests for this Chapter.

Long run	In economic models, the long run time frame assumes no fixed factors of production. Firms can enter or leave the marketplace, and the cost (and availability) of land, labor, raw materials, and capital goods can be assumed to vary.
Consumption	In Keynesian economics consumption refers to personal consumption expenditure, i.e., the purchase of currently produced goods and services out of income, out of savings (net worth), or from borrowed funds. It refers to that part of disposable income that does not go to saving.
Economics	The social science dealing with the use of scarce resources to obtain the maximum satisfaction of society's virtually unlimited economic wants is an economics.
Supply and demand	The partial equilibrium supply and demand economic model originally developed by Alfred Marshall attempts to describe, explain, and predict changes in the price and quantity of goods sold in competitive markets.
Economic theory	Economic theory refers to a statement of a cause-effect relationship; when accepted by all economists, an economic principle.
Fund	Independent accounting entity with a self-balancing set of accounts segregated for the purposes of carrying on specific activities is referred to as a fund.
Pure rate of interest	An essentially risk-free, long-term interest rate that is free of the influence of market imperfections is a pure rate of interest.
Inflation	An increase in the overall price level of an economy, usually as measured by the CPI or by the implicit price deflator is called inflation.
Inefficient market	A market in which prices do not reflect all available information is called an inefficient market.
Deregulation	The lessening or complete removal of government regulations on an industry, especially concerning the price that firms are allowed to charge and leaving price to be determined by market forces a deregulation.
Trend	Trend refers to the long-term movement of an economic variable, such as its average rate of increase or decrease over enough years to encompass several business cycles.
Federal government	Federal government refers to the government of the United States, as distinct from the state and local governments.
Policy	Similar to a script in that a policy can be a less than completely rational decision-making method. Involves the use of a pre-existing set of decision steps for any problem that presents itself.
Fiscal policy	Fiscal policy refers to any macroeconomic policy involving the levels of government purchases, transfers, or taxes, usually implicitly focused on domestic goods, residents, or firms.
Federal Reserve	The Federal Reserve System was created via the Federal Reserve Act of December 23rd, 1913. All national banks were required to join the system and other banks could join. The Reserve Banks opened for business on November 16th, 1914. Federal Reserve Notes were created as part of the legislation, to provide an elastic supply of currency.
Financial transaction	A financial transaction involves a change in the status of the finances of two or more businesses or individuals.
Prime rate	The rate that a bank charges its most creditworthy customers is referred to as the prime rate.
Federal funds	The interest rate banks and other depository institutions charge one another on overnight

Go to **Cram101.com** for the Practice Tests for this Chapter.

rate	loans made out of their excess reserves is called federal funds rate.
Commercial bank	A firm that engages in the business of banking is a commercial bank.
Discount	The difference between the face value of a bond and its selling price, when a bond is sold for less than its face value it's referred to as a discount.
Discount rate	Discount rate refers to the rate, per year, at which future values are diminished to make them comparable to values in the present. Can be either subjective or objective .
Monetary policy	The use of the money supply and/or the interest rate to influence the level of economic activity and other policy objectives including the balance of payments or the exchange rate is called monetary policy.
Yield	The interest rate that equates a future value or an annuity to a given present value is a yield.
Bond	Bond refers to a debt instrument, issued by a borrower and promising a specified stream of payments to the purchaser, usually regular interest payments plus a final repayment of principal.
Basis point	One one-hundredth of a percentage point is a basis point. Each one percent in interest is equal to 100 basis points.
Points	Loan origination fees that may be deductible as interest by a buyer of property. A seller of property who pays points reduces the selling price by the amount of the points paid for the buyer.
Positively correlated	Positively correlated refers to values or amounts of two items that move in the same direction. In accounting and finance, the amount of risk and the amount of return on an investment move in the same direction.
Purchasing	Purchasing refers to the function in a firm that searches for quality material resources, finds the best suppliers, and negotiates the best price for goods and services.
Purchasing power	The amount of goods that money will buy, usually measured by the CPI is referred to as purchasing power.
Nominal rate of interest	The nominal rate of interest is the percentage by which the money the borrower pays back exceeds the money that he borrowed, making no adjustment for any fall in the purchasing power of this money that results from inflation.
Real rate of interest	The real rate of interest is the percentage increase in purchasing power that the borrower pays to the lender for the privilege of borrowing. It is the nominal rate of interest minus the inflation rate.
Correlation	A correlation is the measure of the extent to which two economic or statistical variables move together, normalized so that its values range from -1 to +1. It is defined as the covariance of the two variables divided by the square root of the product of their variances.
Investment	Investment refers to spending for the production and accumulation of capital and additions to inventories. In a financial sense, buying an asset with the expectation of making a return.
Nominal dollars	Nominal dollars refers to the measure used for an actual cash flow that is observed.
Insurance	Insurance refers to a system by which individuals can reduce their exposure to risk of large losses by spreading the risks among a large number of persons.
Consumer price index	Consumer price index refers to a price index for the goods purchased by consumers in an economy, usually based on only a representative sample of typical consumer goods and services. Commonly used to measure inflation. Contrasts with the implicit price deflator.

Go to **Cram101.com** for the Practice Tests for this Chapter.

Price index	A measure of the average prices of a group of goods relative to a base year. A typical price index for a vector of quantities q and prices pb, pg in the base and given years respectively would be I = 100 Pgq / Pbq.
Treasury security	A treasury security is a government bond issued by the United States Department of the Treasury through the Bureau of the Public Debt. They are the debt financing instruments of the U.S. Federal government, and are often referred to simply as Treasuries.
Security	Security refers to a claim on the borrower future income that is sold by the borrower to the lender. A security is a type of transferable interest representing financial value.
Maturity	Maturity refers to the final payment date of a loan or other financial instrument, after which point no further interest or principal need be paid.
Holding	The holding is a court's determination of a matter of law based on the issue presented in the particular case. In other words: under this law, with these facts, this result.
Context	The effect of the background under which a message often takes on more and richer meaning is a context. Context is especially important in cross-cultural interactions because some cultures are said to be high context or low context.
Financial statement	Financial statement refers to a summary of all the transactions that have occurred over a particular period.
Discounted cash flow	In finance, the discounted cash flow approach describes a method to value a project or an entire company. The DCF methods determine the present value of future cash flows by discounting them using the appropriate cost of capital.
Cash flow	In finance, cash flow refers to the amounts of cash being received and spent by a business during a defined period of time, sometimes tied to a specific project. Most of the time they are being used to determine gaps in the liquid position of a company.
Market value	Market value refers to the price of an asset agreed on between a willing buyer and a willing seller; the price an asset could demand if it is sold on the open market.
Mortgage	Mortgage refers to a note payable issued for property, such as a house, usually repaid in equal installments consisting of part principle and part interest, over a specified period.
Corporate bond	A Corporate bond is a bond issued by a corporation, as the name suggests. The term is usually applied to longer term debt instruments, generally with a maturity date falling at least 12 months after their issue date (the term "commercial paper" being sometimes used for instruments with a shorter maturity).
Default	In finance, default occurs when a debtor has not met its legal obligations according to the debt contract, e.g. it has not made a scheduled payment, or violated a covenant (condition) of the debt contract.
Risk premium	In finance, the risk premium can be the expected rate of return above the risk-free interest rate.
Premium	Premium refers to the fee charged by an insurance company for an insurance policy. The rate of losses must be relatively predictable: In order to set the premium (prices) insurers must be able to estimate them accurately.
Probability distribution	A specification of the probabilities for each possible value of a random variable is called probability distribution.
Distribution	Distribution in economics, the manner in which total output and income is distributed among individuals or factors.
Portfolio	In finance, a portfolio is a collection of investments held by an institution or a private

individual. Holding but not always a portfolio is part of an investment and risk-limiting strategy called diversification. By owning several assets, certain types of risk (in particular specific risk) can be reduced.

Mistake	In contract law a mistake is incorrect understanding by one or more parties to a contract and may be used as grounds to invalidate the agreement. Common law has identified three different types of mistake in contract: unilateral mistake, mutual mistake, and common mistake.
Default risk	The chance that the issuer of a debt instrument will be unable to make interest payments or pay off the face value when the instrument matures is called default risk.
Consideration	Consideration in contract law, a basic requirement for an enforceable agreement under traditional contract principles, defined in this text as legal value, bargained for and given in exchange for an act or promise. In corporation law, cash or property contributed to a corporation in exchange for shares, or a promise to contribute such cash or property.
Coupon rate	In bonds, notes or other fixed income securities, the stated percentage rate of interest, usually paid twice a year is the coupon rate.
Coupon	In finance, a coupon is "attached" to a bond, either physically (as with old bonds) or electronically. Each coupon represents a predetermined payment promized to the bond-holder in return for his or her loan of money to the bond-issuer. .
At par	At equality refers to at par. Two currencies are said to be 'at par' if they are trading one-for-one.
Term structure of interest rates	The relationship among interest rates on bonds with different terms to maturity is referred to as term structure of interest rates.
Yield curve	In finance, the yield curve is the relation between the interest rate (or cost of borrowing) and the maturity of the debt for a given borrower in a given currency.
Slope	The slope of a line in the plane containing the x and y axes is generally represented by the letter m, and is defined as the change in the y coordinate divided by the corresponding change in the x coordinate, between two distinct points on the line.
Spot rate	Spot rate refers to the rate at which the currency is traded for immediate delivery. It is the existing cash price.
Internal rate of return	Internal rate of return refers to a discounted cash flow method for evaluating capital budgeting projects. The internal rate of return is a discount rate that makes the present value of the cash inflows equal to the present value of the cash outflows.
Rate of return	A rate of return is a comparison of the money earned (or lost) on an investment to the amount of money invested.
Yield to maturity	Yield to maturity refers to the required rate of return on a bond issue. It is the discount rate used in present-valuing future interest payments and the principal payment at maturity. The term is used interchangeably with market rate of interest.
Forward rate	Forward rate refers to the forward exchange rate, this is the exchange rate on a forward market transaction.
Option	A contract that gives the purchaser the option to buy or sell the underlying financial instrument at a specified price, called the exercise price or strike price, within a specific period of time.
Arbitrage	An arbitrage is a combination of nearly simultaneous transactions designed to profit from an existing discrepancy among prices, exchange rates, and/or interest rates on different markets without assuming risk.

Hedging	A technique for avoiding a risk by making a counteracting transaction is referred to as hedging.
Annuity	A contract to make regular payments to a person for life or for a fixed period is an annuity.
Accounting	A system that collects and processes financial information about an organization and reports that information to decision makers is referred to as accounting.
Interest income	Interest income refers to payments of income to those who supply the economy with capital.
Margin	A deposit by a buyer in stocks with a seller or a stockbroker, as security to cover fluctuations in the market in reference to stocks that the buyer has purchased but for which he has not paid is a margin. Commodities are also traded on margin.
Weighted average	The weighted average unit cost of the goods available for sale for both cost of goods sold and ending inventory.
Volatility	Volatility refers to the extent to which an economic variable, such as a price or an exchange rate, moves up and down over time.
Variance	Variance refers to a measure of how much an economic or statistical variable varies across values or observations. Its calculation is the same as that of the covariance, being the covariance of the variable with itself.
Principal	In agency law, one under whose direction an agent acts and for whose benefit that agent acts is a principal.
Perpetuity	A perpetuity is an annuity in which the periodic payments begin on a fixed date and continue indefinitely. Fixed coupon payments on permanently invested (irredeemable) sums of money are prime examples of perpetuities. Scholarships paid perpetually from an endowment fit the definition of perpetuity.
Dividend	Amount of corporate profits paid out for each share of stock is referred to as dividend.
Stock	In financial terminology, stock is the capital raized by a corporation, through the issuance and sale of shares.
Preferred stock	Stock that has specified rights over common stock is a preferred stock.
Coupon bond	A credit market instrument, the coupon bond pays the owner a fixed interest payment every year until the maturity date, when a specified final amount is repaid.
Zero coupon bond	A zero coupon bond is a bond which do not pay periodic coupons, or so-called "interest payments." They are purchased at a discount from their value at maturity. The holder of a zero coupon bond is entitled to receive a single payment, usually of a specified sum of money at a specified time in the future.
Cash inflow	Cash coming into the company as the result of a previous investment is a cash inflow.
Balance	In banking and accountancy, the outstanding balance is the amount of money owned, (or due), that remains in a deposit account (or a loan account) at a given date, after all past remittances, payments and withdrawal have been accounted for. It can be positive (then, in the balance sheet of a firm, it is an asset) or negative (a liability).
Certificate of deposit	An acknowledgment by a bank of the receipt of money with an engagement to pay it back is referred to as certificate of deposit.
Financial institution	A financial institution acts as an agent that provides financial services for its clients. Financial institutions generally fall under financial regulation from a government authority.
Investment contract	In securities law, a type of security encompassing any contract by which an investor invests in a common enterprise with an expectation of profits solely from the efforts of persons

Go to **Cram101.com** for the Practice Tests for this Chapter.

other than the investor are referred to as investment contract.

Contract	A contract is a "promise" or an "agreement" that is enforced or recognized by the law. In the civil law, a contract is considered to be part of the general law of obligations.
Holder	A person in possession of a document of title or an instrument payable or indorsed to him, his order, or to bearer is a holder.
Cash outflow	Cash flowing out of the business from all sources over a period of time is cash outflow.
Enterprise	Enterprise refers to another name for a business organization. Other similar terms are business firm, sometimes simply business, sometimes simply firm, as well as company, and entity.
Convexity	In finance, convexity is a measure of the sensitivity of the price of a bond to changes in interest rates. It is related to the concept of duration.
Rebalancing	Rebalancing is the action of bringing a portfolio of investments that has deviated away from one's target asset allocation back into line. Under-weighted securities can be purchased with newly saved money; alternatively, over-weighted securities can be sold to purchase under-weighted securities.
Profit	Profit refers to the return to the resource entrepreneurial ability; total revenue minus total cost.
Money market	The money market, in macroeconomics and international finance, refers to the equilibration of demand for a country's domestic money to its money supply; market for short-term financial instruments.
Derivative	A derivative is a generic term for specific types of investments from which payoffs over time are derived from the performance of assets (such as commodities, shares or bonds), interest rates, exchange rates, or indices (such as a stock market index, consumer price index (CPI) or an index of weather conditions).
Matching	Matching refers to an accounting concept that establishes when expenses are recognized. Expenses are matched with the revenues they helped to generate and are recognized when those revenues are recognized.
Normal yield curve	Normal yield curve refers to an upward-sloping yield curve. Long-term interest rates are higher than short-term rates.
Incentive	An incentive is any factor (financial or non-financial) that provides a motive for a particular course of action, or counts as a reason for preferring one choice to the alternatives.
Certificates of deposit	Certificates of deposit refer to a certificate offered by banks, savings and loans, and other financial institutions for the deposit of funds at a given interest rate over a specified time period.
Instrument	Instrument refers to an economic variable that is controlled by policy makers and can be used to influence other variables, called targets. Examples are monetary and fiscal policies used to achieve external and internal balance.
Constant Dollars	The term Constant dollars refers to a metric for valuing the price of something over time, without that metric changing due to inflation or deflation. The term specifically refers to dollars whose present value is linked to a given year.
Pension	A pension is a steady income given to a person (usually after retirement). Pensions are typically payments made in the form of a guaranteed annuity to a retired or disabled employee.

Go to **Cram101.com** for the Practice Tests for this Chapter.

Business plan	A detailed written statement that describes the nature of the business, the target market, the advantages the business will have in relation to competition, and the resources and qualifications of the owner is referred to as a business plan.
Mortgage company	Mortgage company refers to a financial institution that lends money to borrowers to purchase property.
Par value	The central value of a pegged exchange rate, around which the actual rate is permitted to fluctuate within set bounds is a par value.
Standard deviation	A measure of the spread or dispersion of a series of numbers around the expected value is the standard deviation. The standard deviation tells us how well the expected value represents a series of values.
Callable bond	A callable bond is a bond that can be redeemed by the issuer prior to its maturity, on certain dates, at a price determined at issuance.
Accumulation	The acquisition of an increasing quantity of something. The accumulation of factors, especially capital, is a primary mechanism for economic growth.
Common stock	Common stock refers to the basic, normal, voting stock issued by a corporation; called residual equity because it ranks after preferred stock for dividend and liquidation distributions.
Exchange	The trade of things of value between buyer and seller so that each is better off after the trade is called the exchange.

Interest	In finance and economics, interest is the price paid by a borrower for the use of a lender's money. In other words, interest is the amount of paid to "rent" money for a period of time.
Present value	The value today of a stream of payments and/or receipts over time in the future and/or the past, converted to the present using an interest rate. If X t is the amount in period t and r the interest rate, then present value at time t=0 is V = ?T /t.
Investment	Investment refers to spending for the production and accumulation of capital and additions to inventories. In a financial sense, buying an asset with the expectation of making a return.
Interest rate	The rate of return on bonds, loans, or deposits. When one speaks of 'the' interest rate, it is usually in a model where there is only one.
Variance	Variance refers to a measure of how much an economic or statistical variable varies across values or observations. Its calculation is the same as that of the covariance, being the covariance of the variable with itself.
Probability density	For a continuous random variable, a function whose integral over any set is the probability of the variable being in that set is referred to as probability density.
Evaluation	The consumer's appraisal of the product or brand on important attributes is called evaluation.
Annuity	A contract to make regular payments to a person for life or for a fixed period is an annuity.
Trial	An examination before a competent tribunal, according to the law of the land, of the facts or law put in issue in a cause, for the purpose of determining such issue is a trial. When the court hears and determines any issue of fact or law for the purpose of determining the rights of the parties, it may be considered a trial.
Standard deviation	A measure of the spread or dispersion of a series of numbers around the expected value is the standard deviation. The standard deviation tells us how well the expected value represents a series of values.
Fund	Independent accounting entity with a self-balancing set of accounts segregated for the purposes of carrying on specific activities is referred to as a fund.
Distribution	Distribution in economics, the manner in which total output and income is distributed among individuals or factors.
Variable	A variable is something measured by a number; it is used to analyze what happens to other things when the size of that number changes.
Random variable	Random variable refers to an economic or statistical variable that takes on multiple values, each with some probability that is specified by a probability distribution.
Appeal	Appeal refers to the act of asking an appellate court to overturn a decision after the trial court's final judgment has been entered.
Moving average	A moving average series can be calculated for any time series, but is most often applied to stock prices, returns or trading volumes. Moving averages are used to smooth out short-term fluctuations, thus highlighting longer-term trends or cycles.
Time series	In statistics and signal processing, a time series is a sequence of data points, measured typically at successive times, spaced at (often uniform) time intervals. Analysts throughout the economy will use these to aid in the management of their corresponding businesses.
Risk premium	In finance, the risk premium can be the expected rate of return above the risk-free interest rate.
Premium	Premium refers to the fee charged by an insurance company for an insurance policy. The rate of losses must be relatively predictable: In order to set the premium (prices) insurers must

Go to **Cram101.com** for the Practice Tests for this Chapter.

	be able to estimate them accurately.
Yield	The interest rate that equates a future value or an annuity to a given present value is a yield.
Portfolio	In finance, a portfolio is a collection of investments held by an institution or a private individual. Holding but not always a portfolio is part of an investment and risk-limiting strategy called diversification. By owning several assets, certain types of risk (in particular specific risk) can be reduced.
Diversification	Investing in a collection of assets whose returns do not always move together, with the result that overall risk is lower than for individual assets is referred to as diversification.
Market risk	Market risk is the risk that the value of an investment will decrease due to moves in market factors.
Market	A market is, as defined in economics, a social arrangement that allows buyers and sellers to discover information and carry out a voluntary exchange of goods or services.
Systematic risk	Movements in a stock portfolio's value that are attributable to macroeconomic forces affecting all firms in an economy, rather than factors specific to an individual firm are referred to as systematic risk.
Capital asset pricing model	The capital asset pricing model is used in finance to determine a theoretically appropriate required rate of return (and thus the price if expected cash flows can be estimated) of an asset, if that asset is to be added to an already well-diversified portfolio, given that asset's non-diversifiable risk.
Capital asset	In accounting, a capital asset is an asset that is recorded as property that creates more property, e.g. a factory that creates shoes, or a forest that yields a quantity of wood.
Capital	Capital generally refers to financial wealth, especially that used to start or maintain a business. In classical economics, capital is one of four factors of production, the others being land and labor and entrepreneurship.
Asset	An item of property, such as land, capital, money, a share in ownership, or a claim on others for future payment, such as a bond or a bank deposit is an asset.
Common stock	Common stock refers to the basic, normal, voting stock issued by a corporation; called residual equity because it ranks after preferred stock for dividend and liquidation distributions.
Stock	In financial terminology, stock is the capital raized by a corporation, through the issuance and sale of shares.
Security	Security refers to a claim on the borrower future income that is sold by the borrower to the lender. A security is a type of transferable interest representing financial value.
Cash flow	In finance, cash flow refers to the amounts of cash being received and spent by a business during a defined period of time, sometimes tied to a specific project. Most of the time they are being used to determine gaps in the liquid position of a company.
Discount	The difference between the face value of a bond and its selling price, when a bond is sold for less than its face value it's referred to as a discount.
Expected value	A representative value from a probability distribution arrived at by multiplying each outcome by the associated probability and summing up the values is called the expected value.
Market price	Market price is an economic concept with commonplace familiarity; it is the price that a good or service is offered at, or will fetch, in the marketplace; it is of interest mainly in the

study of microeconomics.

Liability	A liability is a present obligation of the enterprise arizing from past events, the settlement of which is expected to result in an outflow from the enterprise of resources embodying economic benefits.
Insurance	Insurance refers to a system by which individuals can reduce their exposure to risk of large losses by spreading the risks among a large number of persons.
Dividend	Amount of corporate profits paid out for each share of stock is referred to as dividend.
Call price	Call price refers to specified price that must be paid for bonds that are called; usually higher than the face amount of the bonds.
Exercise price	Exercise price refers to the price at which the purchaser of an option has the right to buy or sell the underlying financial instrument. Also known as the strike price.
Points	Loan origination fees that may be deductible as interest by a buyer of property. A seller of property who pays points reduces the selling price by the amount of the points paid for the buyer.
Treasury security	A treasury security is a government bond issued by the United States Department of the Treasury through the Bureau of the Public Debt. They are the debt financing instruments of the U.S. Federal government, and are often referred to simply as Treasuries.
Yield curve	In finance, the yield curve is the relation between the interest rate (or cost of borrowing) and the maturity of the debt for a given borrower in a given currency.
Arbitrage	An arbitrage is a combination of nearly simultaneous transactions designed to profit from an existing discrepancy among prices, exchange rates, and/or interest rates on different markets without assuming risk.
Profit	Profit refers to the return to the resource entrepreneurial ability; total revenue minus total cost.
Hedging	A technique for avoiding a risk by making a counteracting transaction is referred to as hedging.
Option	A contract that gives the purchaser the option to buy or sell the underlying financial instrument at a specified price, called the exercise price or strike price, within a specific period of time.
Financial instrument	Formal or legal documents in writing, such as contracts, deeds, wills, bonds, leases, and mortgages is referred to as a financial instrument.
Instrument	Instrument refers to an economic variable that is controlled by policy makers and can be used to influence other variables, called targets. Examples are monetary and fiscal policies used to achieve external and internal balance.
Exchange	The trade of things of value between buyer and seller so that each is better off after the trade is called the exchange.
Callable bond	A callable bond is a bond that can be redeemed by the issuer prior to its maturity, on certain dates, at a price determined at issuance.
Bond	Bond refers to a debt instrument, issued by a borrower and promising a specified stream of payments to the purchaser, usually regular interest payments plus a final repayment of principal.
Call option	Call option refers to an option contract that provides the right to buy a security at a specified price within a certain time period.

Go to **Cram101.com** for the Practice Tests for this Chapter.
And, **NEVER** highlight a book again!

Random walk	The movements of a variable whose future changes cannot be predicted because the variable is just as likely to fall as to rise from today's value is called a random walk.
Rate of return	A rate of return is a comparison of the money earned (or lost) on an investment to the amount of money invested.
Balance	In banking and accountancy, the outstanding balance is the amount of money owned, (or due), that remains in a deposit account (or a loan account) at a given date, after all past remittances, payments and withdrawal have been accounted for. It can be positive (then, in the balance sheet of a firm, it is an asset) or negative (a liability).
Expected return	Expected return refers to the return on an asset expected over the next period.
Cash outflow	Cash flowing out of the business from all sources over a period of time is cash outflow.
Cash inflow	Cash coming into the company as the result of a previous investment is a cash inflow.
Consideration	Consideration in contract law, a basic requirement for an enforceable agreement under traditional contract principles, defined in this text as legal value, bargained for and given in exchange for an act or promise. In corporation law, cash or property contributed to a corporation in exchange for shares, or a promise to contribute such cash or property.
Frequency	Frequency refers to the speed of the up and down movements of a fluctuating economic variable; that is, the number of times per unit of time that the variable completes a cycle of up and down movement.
Analyst	Analyst refers to a person or tool with a primary function of information analysis, generally with a more limited, practical and short term set of goals than a researcher.
Volatility	Volatility refers to the extent to which an economic variable, such as a price or an exchange rate, moves up and down over time.
Trend	Trend refers to the long-term movement of an economic variable, such as its average rate of increase or decrease over enough years to encompass several business cycles.
Secular trend	Secular trend refers to a long-term tendency; a change in some variable over a very long period of years.
Depression	Depression refers to a prolonged period characterized by high unemployment, low output and investment, depressed business confidence, falling prices, and widespread business failures. A milder form of business downturn is a recession.
Hyperinflation	Hyperinflation refers to a very rapid rise in the price level; an extremely high rate of inflation.
Mistake	In contract law a mistake is incorrect understanding by one or more parties to a contract and may be used as grounds to invalidate the agreement. Common law has identified three different types of mistake in contract: unilateral mistake, mutual mistake, and common mistake.
Common mistake	A common mistake is where both parties hold the same mistaken belief of the facts.
Investment contract	In securities law, a type of security encompassing any contract by which an investor invests in a common enterprise with an expectation of profits solely from the efforts of persons other than the investor are referred to as investment contract.
Contract	A contract is a "promise" or an "agreement" that is enforced or recognized by the law. In the civil law, a contract is considered to be part of the general law of obligations.
Credit	Credit refers to a recording as positive in the balance of payments, any transaction that gives rise to a payment into the country, such as an export, the sale of an asset, or borrowing from abroad.

Go to **Cram101.com** for the Practice Tests for this Chapter.

Future interest	Future interest refers to an interest that will come into being at some future time. It is distinguished from a present interest, which already exists. Assume that Dan transfers securities to a newly created trust.
Term structure of interest rates	The relationship among interest rates on bonds with different terms to maturity is referred to as term structure of interest rates.
Contribution	In business organization law, the cash or property contributed to a business by its owners is referred to as contribution.
Extension	Extension refers to an out-of-court settlement in which creditors agree to allow the firm more time to meet its financial obligations. A new repayment schedule will be developed, subject to the acceptance of creditors.
Matching	Matching refers to an accounting concept that establishes when expenses are recognized. Expenses are matched with the revenues they helped to generate and are recognized when those revenues are recognized.
Futures	Futures refer to contracts for the sale and future delivery of stocks or commodities, wherein either party may waive delivery, and receive or pay, as the case may be, the difference in market price at the time set for delivery.
Firm	An organization that employs resources to produce a good or service for profit and owns and operates one or more plants is referred to as a firm.
Market risk premium	Market risk premium refers to a premium over and above the risk-free rate. It is represented by the difference between the market return and the risk-free rate, and it may be multiplied by the beta coefficient to determine the additional risk-adjusted return on a security.
Par value	The central value of a pegged exchange rate, around which the actual rate is permitted to fluctuate within set bounds is a par value.
At par	At equality refers to at par. Two currencies are said to be 'at par' if they are trading one-for-one.
Coupon	In finance, a coupon is "attached" to a bond, either physically (as with old bonds) or electronically. Each coupon represents a predetermined payment promized to the bond-holder in return for his or her loan of money to the bond-issuer. .
Corporate bond	A Corporate bond is a bond issued by a corporation, as the name suggests. The term is usually applied to longer term debt instruments, generally with a maturity date falling at least 12 months after their issue date (the term "commercial paper" being sometimes used for instruments with a shorter maturity).
Spot rate	Spot rate refers to the rate at which the currency is traded for immediate delivery. It is the existing cash price.